transparent living

living a life of integrity

Rod Handley

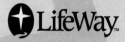

LifeWay Christian Resources
Nashville, Tennessee

Produced by: National Student Ministry Department

LifeWay Christian Resources • 127 Ninth Avenue North • Nashville, Tennessee 37234 • Customer Service: (800) 458-2772

Dewey Decimal Classification: 170

Subject Heading: Integrity/Christian Life

This study is based on *Character Counts: Who's Counting Yours?* by Rod Handley. Published by Cross Training Publishing, Grand Island, Nebraska.

ISBN 0-7673-9296-5

INTEGRITY

contents

about the writers 4

the crossseekers covenant 5

session one
living a life of integrity. 6

session two
integrity in daily living 20

session three
integrity in relationships 34

session four
integrity in school and work 48

session five
integrity in the hidden things 60

session six
integrity through accountability groups 74

leader's guide 88

crossseekers resources 93

transparentliving

living a life of integrity

about the writers

Rod Handley is chief operating officer and chief financial officer for the Fellowship of Christian Athletes. Rod has served with FCA since 1986, initially serving in the state of Washington before joining the national office in Kansas City, Missouri, in 1989. Prior to his work with FCA, Rod was a certified public accountant for Ernst and Whinney. Rod is the author of *Character Counts: Who's Counting Yours?* which is the foundation for this study. Rod, his wife, Janna, and their three children live in Kansas City.

David McDurham wrote the interactive aspects of *Transparent Living.* David is College Minister at First Baptist Church of Arlington, Texas. He lives in Fort Worth with his wife, Amy Myers McDurham. A native of Tennessee, David graduated from Tennessee Tech University in 1992 and Southwestern Baptist Theological Seminary in 1995. While a student, he was active in both church college ministry and the Baptist Student Union. Along with collegiate ministry, he enjoys spending time with friends and traveling to Tennessee to visit family.

The CrossSeekers™ Covenant

"You will seek me and find me when you seek me with all your heart." Jeremiah 29:13

As a seeker of the cross of Christ, I am called to break away from trite, nonchalant, laissez-faire Christian living. I accept the challenge to divine daring, to consecrated recklessness for Christ, to devout adventure in the face of ridiculing contemporaries. Created in the image of God and committed to excellence as a disciple of Jesus Christ,

I will be a person of integrity

"Do your best to present yourself to God as one approved, a workman who does not need to be ashamed and who correctly handles the word of truth." 2 Timothy 2:15

My attitudes and actions reveal my commitment to live the kind of life Christ modeled for me—to speak the truth in love, to stand firm in my convictions, to be honest and trustworthy.

I will pursue consistent spiritual growth

"So then, just as you received Christ Jesus as Lord, continue to live in him, rooted and built up in him, strengthened in the faith as you were taught, and overflowing with thankfulness." Colossians 2:6-7

The Christian life is a continuing journey, and I am committed to a consistent, personal relationship with Jesus Christ, to faithful study of His Word, and to regular corporate spiritual growth through the ministry of the New Testament church.

I will speak and live a relevant, authentic, and consistent witness

"Always be prepared to give an answer to everyone who asks you to give the reason for the hope that you have." 1 Peter 3:15

I will tell others the story of how Jesus changed my life, and I will seek to live a radically changed life each day. I will share the good news of Jesus Christ with courage and boldness.

I will seek opportunities to serve in Christ's name

"The Spirit of the Lord is on me, because he has anointed me to preach good news to the poor. He has sent me to proclaim freedom for the prisoners and recovery of sight for the blind, to release the oppressed, to proclaim the year of the Lord's favor." Luke 4:18-19

I believe that God desires to draw all people into a loving, redeeming relationship with Him. As His disciple, I will give myself to be His hands to reach others in ministry and missions.

I will honor my body as the temple of God, dedicated to a lifestyle of purity

"Do you not know that your body is a temple of the Holy Spirit, who is in you, whom you have received from God? You are not your own; you were bought at a price. Therefore honor God with your body." 1 Corinthians 6:19-20

Following the example of Christ, I will keep my body healthy and strong, avoiding temptations and destructive personal vices. I will honor the gift of life by keeping myself sexually pure and free from addictive drugs.

I will be godly in all things, Christlike in all relationships

"Therefore, as God's chosen people, holy and dearly loved, clothe yourselves with compassion, kindness, humility, gentleness and patience. Bear with each other and forgive whatever grievances you may have against one another. Forgive as the Lord forgave you. And over all these virtues put on love, which binds them all together in perfect unity." Colossians 3:12-14

In every relationship and in every situation, I will seek to live as Christ would. I will work to heal brokenness, to value each person as a child of God, to avoid petty quarrels and harsh words, to let go of bitterness and resentment that hinder genuine Christian love.

integrity

Integrity? Who Cares?

Sal had always been "the man." He excelled far above his peers in academics, athletics, social contacts. Sal had a 4.0 GPA and was first in his high school class. He dominated in athletics, and was named all-state in three sports. He was popular, smooth, and savvy. He got everything he wanted, including his pick of girls. It was no surprise that after graduating from college with honors, he made his mark on the business world. In a few short years, he flew through the ranks and was named president of an international, multimillion-dollar organization. He and his wife traveled the world and lived a life of luxury. They had money and power. Because Sal was recognized worldwide, people applauded when he was named secretary of state. Outwardly Sal had it all. But deep inside, he felt an empty discontent he could not explain.

Joe, on the other hand, grew up with a series of bad breaks. Abused by his brothers at an early age, he spent his adolescent years in a foster home. Through great determination, he rose above what seemed insurmountable odds. His exceptional work ethic caught the attention of his boss, who gave him a substantial promotion. Joe had great power at his fingertips. Several nights while working late on a special project, the boss' very attractive wife visited with unwanted and repeated sexual advances. Joe resisted her. Imagine the shock in the office when federal agents entered Joe's workplace and arrested him for sexual harassment. He sat in jail trying to sort out his life.

Preston built a huge mega-church ministry from scratch. People flocked to hear this eloquent spiritual giant. As one of the most in-demand speakers in America, he traveled frequently, spending many nights away from home. One lonely evening, in a city where he wasn't recognized, Preston slipped out of his hotel in the wee hours of the night into a topless bar. Although he intended this first encounter to be his last, Preston began sliding deeper into the addiction of sexual misconduct. At his lowest point, Preston sat in a peep booth only hours before addressing a large evangelical gathering. When he walked onto the stage, all he could see in his mind was the nameless woman who had just entertained him.

SESSION 1

living a life of integrity

Each of these men faced crises. Sal had all the external signs of success, but it was only a matter of time before an independent counsel uncovered criminal offenses, and he resigned. Joe spent many years in jail before a fellow prisoner put in a good word with some powerful people. The facts came out, and the jury threw out the case against him. Years later he was elected governor. Eventually he was joyously reunited with his brothers and father. Preston, after a ten-year battle with pornography, decided to come clean and reveal his secret struggle.

Perhaps you've recognized that Sal and Joe are fictionalized versions of the biblical characters Saul and Joseph. On the surface Saul was the obvious choice for a king, but his true character eventually revealed itself. Joseph was a spoiled and cocky teenager who chose to make the kind of honest changes that made him a true leader. Unfortunately, Preston's story is not fiction.

What bothers you most about people like Sal, Joe, Joe's boss, the boss' wife, or Preston?
(Circle three and jot down why.)
They're spoiled.
They're lazy.
They're sneaky.
They're greedy.
They're selfish.
They're egotistical.
They abuse self and others.
They're opportunists—taking advantage of people when it benefits them.
They're deceptive.
They're only happy when in the spotlight.
They do right or wrong for the attention it brings them.
They do the right thing only when someone is watching.
They_____.

God knows this lack of consistency annoys us. More importantly, it disappoints Him. Integrity means what's on the inside matches what's on the outside. Saul, Joseph, and Preston illustrate that "Man looks at the outward appearance, but the Lord looks at the heart" (1 Sam. 16:7).

His Word says it like this:

"Do what is right and good in the Lord's sight" (Deut. 6:18).

"Blessed are they who maintain justice, who constantly do what is right" (Ps. 106:3).

"Be careful to do what is right in the eyes of everybody" (Rom. 12:17b).

"Never tire of doing what is right" (2 Thess. 3:13).

"For we are taking pains to do what is right, not only in the eyes of the Lord but also in the eyes of men" (2 Cor. 8:21).

Think of someone who professed to be a Christian but fell into inappropriate behavior. Jot that experience here without identifying details:

Why did this bother you?

Which of the following did you feel, and what did it take to get over it?
• Betrayal:
• Abandonment:
• Lied to:
• Used:
• _____:

Integrity? What Is it, Really?

Merriam-Webster's Collegiate Dictionary defines integrity as "firm adherence to a code of esp. moral or artistic values; the quality or state of being complete or undivided." Integrity comes from the root word integer, meaning whole or entire. An integer is a whole number, one not fractioned in any way. Integrity means whole, entire, complete, and intact. God is into making integers. Satan is into making fractions. God wants to put all the pieces together; Satan wants to take you apart and divide you. He wants to sectionalize you and make you inconsistent. Integrity is a strong sense of right and wrong, and courageously choosing right no matter what the circumstances.

Daniel Taylor describes it like this: "Character [integrity] is not something you have; it is something you are that inevitably shows itself in what you do. It is determined by the stories of which you are a part."

We express disappointment with persons who have let us down and admiration for persons who appear to show integrity. But stop a minute and ponder your own integrity. Rate each of these integrity issues when people are watching you. (1 to 10 in the first column, with 1 being you never express them and 10 being you always express them. This is private—don't show it to your group.)

____ ____ I tell the truth.

____ ____ I avoid half-truths or outright lies that put me in a better light to others.

____ ____ I do my 100 percent best at school.

____ ____ I do my 100 percent best at work.

____ ____ I choose friends with integrity and spend quality time with them.

____ ____ I spend quality relationship time with family.

____ ____ I find ways to serve God no matter where I am or whom I'm with.

____ ____ I stay completely above reproach in financial dealings.

____ ____ I refuse lustful thoughts and attitudes when they come into my head.

____ ____ I stay away from images and other explicit materials that do not glorify God.

____ ____ I consistently show people what Jesus is like by the way I treat them.

____ ____ I take care of my body through exercise, proper eating, proper sleeping.

____ ____ I refuse to allow any person or circumstance rob me of my joy.

Now go back and give a second rating in the second column, this time on how often you express these character virtues when no one is watching you.

Ouch. Not quite so easy to take a look inside. And not as easy to be honest. That's why we need Christ to help us.

Before you go further in this study, ask yourself: Am I certain I know Christ as my personal Savior? True integrity begins in being right with God.

The following quiz can help you evaluate your personal relationship to God. Place a check in the box beside each statement to which you can answer yes.

❑ I believe the Bible, God's Word, is our guide to salvation and eternal life.
❑ I believe the Bible when it tells me I am a sinner and that the penalty for sin is eternal separation from God.
❑ I believe that Jesus is the Son of God, that He died on the cross to pay the penalty for my sin, and that He rose from the grave to provide new life for all who place their faith in Him.

Did you answer yes to each question? Do you want to have eternal life? The Bible tells how to have eternal life.

- **Repent.** Jesus said, "But unless you repent, you too will all perish" (Luke 13:3). Repentance means that you turn from your sin-centered life and yield your life to Christ.
- **Believe.** The Bible says, "For it is by grace you have been saved, through faith—and this not from yourselves, it is the gift of God" (Eph. 2:8). This means that you trust only Jesus to save you. You make Him your Savior and Lord.

If you take these steps—repent and believe—you will have personal salvation in Jesus Christ. Call on Him in prayer right now. Simply pray, "Lord Jesus, I confess that I am a sinner and ask You to forgive me for my sins. Please come into my heart to save me and take control of my life. Thank You for being my Savior and Lord. Amen." [1]

> *Being held accountable to someone implies we are open to questions, vulnerable, and able to objectively listen to encouragement and constructive criticism. Accountability helps us pursue integrity and enables us to be the God-honoring Christians we desire to be.*

Then share your decision with a pastor or Christian friend. Seek to grow in your faith through regular Bible study, prayer, worship, service, and Christian fellowship.

Living a life of integrity begins with being right with God. After you're sure of your relationship with Him, then a next step to living out integrity is becoming accountable for it. Accountability is crucial to living a life of integrity.

But I Don't Need Anyone to Keep Me Accountable!

Many Christians think they can live the Christian life without help from other believers. None of us sets out to entrap himself. None of us plans to build a secret life. We just let one compromise lead to another. We assume that what we choose day to day is nobody's business but our own. King David thought so, too. Read 2 Samuel 11 for an account of his experience.

On a scale of 1 to 10, with 10 being totally honorable, what level of integrity did David display and why?

What was David's first sin? How could he have stopped there?

What was David's next sin? How could he have stopped there?

How did David try to use Uriah?

How did David push Uriah even further?

How did David pull Joab into the deceptive sin pattern?

How did David try to cover up his sin?

Nobody Will Ever Know!

Secrecy is an enemy of integrity. We may assume if no one knows our sin, there's no problem. And though God knows, He understands, we think. Besides, we're strong enough Christians that a little wrongdoing won't matter much. And if it does matter, we can always obtain forgiveness.

Was this how David felt? Despite numerous opportunities to come clean, David sank deeper and deeper into wrongdoing. Did he assume he wouldn't get caught?

Notice the way David responded to Uriah's integrity. Because David had been secretly sinning, he tried to pull Uriah, unknowing, into his devious plan. But Uriah chose the path of integrity. Perhaps he and his fellow soldiers felt a sense of accountability to each other. With accountability, even the king couldn't make Uriah go against his integrity.

How does a person like Uriah have more power than a person like David? Cite both a verse from 2 Samuel 11 and your own experience:

Three incidents from David's experience can help us in our own quest for integrity:

Second Samuel 11:1 tells us that spring was the time kings normally went off to war. But King David sent his soldiers out with Joab while he stayed behind. One key to a successful, integrity-filled walk with Christ is insuring we are always where we need to be, both physically and spiritually.

How can you make sure you are where you need to be spiritually at all times?

Secrecy is an enemy of integrity.

2. The first ten chapters of 2 Samuel focus on the successes of David's reign. Had the successes gone to David's head? What made him think he could get away with these sins?

How do we convince ourselves that we cannot be caught in our sin? How do we rationalize it in our minds? Name three things we tell ourselves:

    1.

    2.

    3.

How could accountability help?

3. Read 2 Samuel 12. Nathan led David to confession and forgiveness. This was critical. But his problems weren't over. Forgiveness didn't remove the consequences of his behavior. True, David healed, but just as cuts leave scars on our skin, sin leaves lasting effects. We don't deliberately set out to sin, but it happens. When we do sin, the best thing to do is get right with God.

Why does every Christian need accountability? Let Hebrews 3:12-13 help you answer this question.

hard-hearted

Hard-hearted? Not Me!

Reread Hebrews 3:12-13. Name a way you have grown hardened, or could grow hardened, by sin's deceitfulness in these areas:

What you say to people:

Movies:

How you spend your time:

Reading material:

Your thought life:

Other: _____:

So, How Do I Show Integrity?

Ultimately, integrity is a willingness to do as God commanded us to do—to consistently love one another as we love ourselves. But agreeing to that is much easier than actually doing it. Consider the actions these persons have taken to live with integrity:

• A former roommate of mine, who played 10 years in the NFL, chose not to read the newspapers after he played a game. Through both successes and failures, he'd learned not to rely on press clippings to determine his value. He said, "I'm not nearly as good or bad as the press believes." He graciously handled praise, realizing he was only a few bad plays away from the "boo" birds.

• Billy Graham exemplifies awareness in a sinful world. Early on in his ministry, Graham decided he would remain faithful to his wife and demonstrate integrity in his relationships. He chooses never to eat a meal with a woman who is not a family member without a third person present. He chooses never to let a woman in his hotel room for any reason, even if that person is a trusted co-worker. He has aides enter a room first to make certain no one is already there when he arrives. Because of these decisions, Graham is one of the few widely known Christian leaders who has not fallen into the heady pit of sexual or other temptation. The impact he has made on millions of people worldwide is lasting and positive.

• My friend Don Hilkemeier chooses to practice integrity by blessing people without fanfare: "I'm going to do something nice for someone, and if they find out, it doesn't count."

What steps of integrity could you take, beginning today, to protect yourself from temptation and to make certain your impact on others is positive? Note one in each of these areas:
Honesty:
Work:
Friendships and dating:
Sexual conduct:
Money:
Family:

Here are a few specific ideas to get you started: [2]

- Be on time.

- Return extra change at the grocery store.

- Set priorities that honor God, family, country, and then career.

- Tell a friend that you can't stop for a drink after work.

- Set a good example— even if it requires playing a difficult and unfamiliar role.

- Honor your commitments.

- Go to a family event such as your sibling's little league game or dance recital.

- Choose the harder right, instead of the easier wrong.

- Accept both good and bad consequences of your actions.

- Be selfless rather than selfish.

- Be accountable to at least one person for your actions.

- Be truthful in all things, while being sensitive to the fact that sometimes the truth hurts and need not be spoken.

- Sacrifice personal pleasures, if necessary, to provide for the well-being of the family.

- Be committed to the well-being of others even if it is personally costly.

- Keep appointments.

Encourage Your Group: Actions for Group Study

1. Develop a definition of integrity that all group members can agree on:

2. Why does almost every person on the planet care about integrity when it comes to the way they are treated?

3. Listen to the "Ragamuffin Intro" about atheism on DC Talk's CD *Jesus Freak* (Forefront, 1995). What damage is done when professing Christians don't demonstrate integrity?

What power is displayed when they do?

4. Do you remember Elaine's boyfriend, Puddy, on *Seinfeld*? He had an Icthus fish symbol on his car, and all the radio presets in his car were tuned to Christian stations. But Puddy's life didn't demonstrate a growing walk with Christ. He was involved in immoral relationships and dealt dishonestly in his car business. Simply stated, he didn't have integrity. Describe another person in movies or on TV who gives a skewed picture of Christianity.

Name someone who gives an accurate picture of Christian integrity.

5. Some people say we have no right to meddle in other people's lives; that what Sal, Joe, Preston, media stars, politicians, and the Christian next to you does is their own business. Do you agree or disagree, and why?

How does what you do in private impact what you do in public?

6. How are you like and unlike David? How are you like and unlike Uriah?

7. Now that we've theorized a bit, let's put the truth into practice. Read again the Bible passages under "Integrity? Who Cares?" Choose one to embrace as your integrity motto (or select another not listed).

8. Keeping your Scripture motto in mind, name a specific way to show integrity in these situations. You'll find starter ideas under "So, How Do I Show Integrity?" Try not to repeat ideas.

- in your dorm or apartment
- in the classroom
- in the cafeteria or bookstore
- when out with friends
- at church

9. Why do you think "I will be a person of integrity" is the first of the CrossSeekers six Covenant points?

Between You and God

1. We'd all like to think that our faith is enough to help us live the Christian life. Why do you need accountability to other Christians?

2. What's the main reason you resist accountability?

3. What's the main reason you want accountability?

4. Why are you more prone to sin if you think no one will find out?

5. Which of the integrity issues under "Integrity? What Is It, Really?" are most critical to you right now? Ask God to give you one starter action to address each.

6. How have you hurt someone by your lack of integrity? Be specific.

How have you hurt God by your lack of integrity? Be specific.

7. How have you helped someone by demonstrating integrity?

How have you honored God by demonstrating integrity?

8. Talk with God about a time you were overwhelmed by a sin, and you didn't feel you could talk to anyone about it. Invite Him to give you an action plan to stay out of a similar trap now and in the future.

9. What delights you about letting God deepen your personal integrity? Talk with Him about that in this space:

10. Complete the following sentences:

When I consider my integrity, I know I need to. . .

The one thing I am going to focus on doing differently this next week is. . .

Notes

1. "The Test of Life," *Collegiate,* Fall 1998, p. 2.
2. "Character—a Definition," Karl Day, *Washington Watch,* November 1997, published by Family Research Council, pp. 1, 7.

integrity

Integrity? I Don't Have Time!

With classes, studying, friends, church, jobs, keeping up a dorm room or apartment, campus activities, fraternities or sororities, and trying to spend time with God, life can get hectic. It seems we never have enough time. We can't participate in every retreat, be active in every club, go to every party, attend every sporting event, study as well as we need to, spend time with God, make time for relaxation and renewal, and attend church. We must make choices.

Unfortunately, what we often omit from our busy schedule is the one thing that will give us strength and ability to make wise decisions: daily quiet time with God. After all, we must turn in our schoolwork, we must attend class, and we must show up for work. But no one knows if we have a daily quiet time.

Maintaining integrity in daily living is difficult during college. Temptations abound. Time pressures are fierce. Many people demand something from us. It's easy to think, "When I finish college, I'll be better in my daily walk with Christ. I'm just so busy right now." I thought this as a college student, too. But my life got even crazier after I graduated. Now I know the key to maintaining personal integrity in daily living is having a daily quiet time with God.

Jeremiah 29:12-13 promises, "Then you will call upon me and come and pray to me, and I will listen to you. You will seek me and find me when you seek me with all your heart." Jesus' life was characterized by earnest devotion to the Father as evidenced by His commitment to arise early in the morning to pray (Mark 1:35). The Son of God realized that even He needed daily fellowship alone with God, and it was a top priority. Now if Jesus Christ needed this time with God, isn't it obvious that we need it as well?

I define quiet time as time alone with God, allowing Him to speak to me through the Bible and communicating with Him through prayer. This intimate time alone with God is the key to deep Christian growth and

maturity. Every committed Christian has this discipline as a core priority.

Establish, renew, or enliven your personal quiet time by giving God quality time before anything else calls for your attention each day. The amount of time you spend is not the most important factor. Invest the first few minutes in preparing your heart in prayer. Then read your Bible. Pick a place to start, and then read consecutively—verse after verse, chapter after chapter. Don't race! Read for the pure joy of reading and allowing God to speak. You may also want to use a devotional book or a Bible study. Set aside the last few minutes of your time for prayer. One easy prayer model is the acrostic ACTS:

- **A—Adoration.** Worship God. Tell the Lord you love Him. Reflect on His greatness, power, majesty, and sovereignty.
- **C—Confession.** After entering His presence and confronting His holiness, He reveals to us our uncleanness. Confess and be cleansed from the sin in your life. The root word of confession means "to agree together with." In confessing, you are agreeing with God on specific sins that you have committed.
- **T—Thanksgiving.** We express gratitude to God. Think of specific things to thank Him for: family, friends, scholarships, job, health, answered prayer, and even hardships.
- **S—Supplication.** To supplicate means to "ask for, earnestly and humbly." Bring your petitions to God, both for others and for yourself.

What does seeking God "with all your heart" mean?

Examine the following definitions of the word *all:*
- each and every thing
- everything one has
- wholly
- exclusively

How does your understanding of the phrase "seek me with all your heart" change after reading these definitions?

What implications does this give for your walk with Christ?

Name 10 things that fill your daily routine. Over the next several days invite God during your quiet time to give you direction on how He wants you to spend your time.

1.
2.
3.
4.
5.
6.
7.
8.
9.
10.

quiet time

Suggestions for Invigorating Your Quiet Time

Maybe you're already having a quiet time, but it's become dry. Here are some ideas to breathe new life into your time with God.

1. **Read for inspiration.** A devotion is meant to be an inspiration in your walk with Christ for that particular day, not an in-depth study of a passage or book.

2. **Don't take copious notes.** Save this for specific study sessions. Try to record one or two insights or promises that God gives you daily. You will soon have a bundle of precious jewels from God. These can be valuable in times of need and spiritual dryness.

3. **Have variety.** It is not necessary to do it exactly the same way every day. Have a plan, but feel free to vary.

4. **Be consistent.** Some days you may not feel like having a quiet time. Do your best to even have just a short one, even if it is just reviewing passages that God impressed on you in weeks and months before.

5. **Read with your mind open to God.** He will surprise you with insights and keen ideas and lead you to do some things you never thought you could or would do. Just give Him a chance.

6. **Expect a blessing.** You will receive this blessing if it is not just a legalistic ritual, but a personal, intimate fellowship with Almighty God. God desires your fellowship; He longs for it. And He will honor your willingness to spend time with Him.

7. **Pray before you read.** Ask God to give you wisdom and concentration in your reading. Then read and pray through the Scripture.

8. **Get it on your schedule.** If your regular time is early in the morning, then be committed to it. Satan would love to squeeze it out of your day when numerous other activities consume you. When you do blow it, confess it, forget it, and renew your commitment to get back on track the next day.

9. **Make notes about passages or topics you want to study more at a later date.** Then go back to these lists and do it!

10. **Meditate on what you read.** A good way to keep in mind what you read is to check up on yourself throughout the day. I often ask myself, "What did I read in my quiet time today?" If you have difficulty recalling it, then you are not retaining it.

11. **Remember the importance of spiritual food.** Through the nourishing of your soul, you literally "eat God's Word." Your spiritual strength is directly related to your intake of the Word.

12. **Enjoy it.** Your quiet time should not be legalistic or drudgery.

It's Just the Beginning

Establishing a quiet time is critical to living a life of integrity. Don't complete your day without spending time with God. Consider how accountability can help you maintain this critical discipline. Teamwork is a concept that God has stressed since the beginning of time:

- In the Garden of Eden, God saw that man needed a suitable helper.
- Moses had his brother Aaron and sister Miriam to help him lead people out of Egypt toward the Promised Land.
- David and Jonathan had a special friendship that encouraged and challenged each.
- Nathan confronted David about his sin with Bathsheba.
- Daniel had three close friends, Shadrach, Meshach, and Abednego, to stand beside him.
- Paul had Barnabus, Silas, and Timothy as companions and co-workers.
- Even Jesus had twelve disciples, and close, intimate friendships with Peter, James, and John.

In fact, if we examine the Bible for people who successfully lived out their faith alone, we will find none. Being sent out two by two has always been a biblical pattern. No person can or is meant to live the Christian life alone. Eventually, our hearts will turn toward evil. Jeremiah 17:9 says, "The heart is deceitful above all things and beyond cure. Who can understand it?"

God never intended for us to live out our Christianity as a "lone ranger." Even the television character Lone Ranger had his sidekick Tonto and his beloved horse Silver. "Two are better than one, because they have a good return for their work: If one falls down, his friend can help him up," and "A cord of three strands is not quickly broken," states Ecclesiastes 4:10, 12.

Biblical examples abound of people getting into trouble because they tried to go it on their own. What trouble did these Bible characters create for themselves? (In addition to the verses you remember, use a Bible concordance to look up others.)

- **Adam and Eve:**
- **Cain:**
- **Esau:**
- **Reuben:**
- **Moses:**

- **Samson:**
- **Saul:**
- **Judas:**
- **Ananias and Sapphira:**
- **David:**

Because "the heart is deceitful above all things" we can be easily deceived. When we know someone knows, when we report to someone, when we must explain our actions, we are more likely to do the right thing.

Tell about a time you were deceived in:
- A relationship:
- A friendship:
- Leadership:
- Ego:
- A choice:
- Other: _____:

Did another Christian help you see things clearly? How did he prompt you to make needed changes?

I'm Still Not Convinced

Certainly those Bible characters fell. You might say, "But I have them as examples. I won't make the same mistakes." But we have one big strike against us—we're sinful human beings. All of us sin, especially when we try to live life on our own. Other Christians help us be mindful that we're all sinners (Rom. 3:23).

Here are five reasons every Christian needs accountability:

1. Satan, our enemy, loves to see us stumble.

It brings great pleasure to Satan to see us fall. Every believer is a target. Satan uses many methods, but two of his favorite and trickiest ways are:

- Convincing us we can do something on our own.
- Injecting distractions in our weakest areas, especially when we have idle time on our hands.

Read these passages and note strategies for defeating Satan (be specific):

1 Peter 5:8-9

Ephesians 6:11, 13-18

Colossians 3:2-10

2. The world is closely watching us.

God commands us to be holy because He is holy (I Pet. 1:16). This purity shows the world what God is like. We are the only Jesus some people may ever see. We aren't perfect, but when we obey Christ, people notice. Many are attracted to Him by observing our actions and words. But many more are repelled when they see us living hypocritical lives.

Read Matthew 5:16 to discover two results in choosing to walk in the light:

Tell how you have seen these results in your own life or in the life of someone you know:

Holiness is manifested in our lives as God transforms us. We begin to change from the inside out. Here are some questions to discover whether or not you are walking in the light of holiness:

- Does my life honor God? Or am I focusing on putting forth an image?
- What picture does my life present of Jesus? Is it an accurate picture? Is it a shallow one, or does it go deep?
- What do those closest to me say about my character—how well does what they say match how I am on the inside?
- How will I act with integrity when I don't feel like it?
- Do my motives match God's purposes?

3. To remain right with the Lord.

God has done a complete work in us, as described in Ephesians 2:4-10. He loves us. This love has been demonstrated to us time and time again, even when we fail miserably in returning that love to Him. His love for us is further demonstrated by God"s willingness to send Jesus to earth to die for us (Rom. 5:8). He paid a significant price for us through His shed blood, and we have the opportunity to spend eternity with Him by accepting Christ. When we also consider His power and forgiveness in our lives, I must ask, "Why blow it?" Living pure, holy, and blameless should be a goal for every believer.

Why were you created? Answer this in terms a non-believer can understand.

4. Judgment is coming.

Former New York Yankee Mickey Mantle died several years ago. At his funeral, broadcaster Bob Costas shared these words: "Our last memories of Mickey Mantle are as heroic as the first. None of us, Mickey included, would want to be held accountable for every moment of our lives." In many ways Bob was right. I'd like to go my own independent way, never having to give an accounting for my actions and behaviors. But the cold, hard reality is: God will judge (Eccl. 12:14). There will be a full accounting of our lives and all will be revealed. Accountability will help prepare you for that day.

Are you ready to face a holy God? Why or why not?

5. Accountability encourages us.

It feels wonderful to gather with people who really love and accept us, who are willing to talk with us honestly and help keep us on the "straight and narrow" path. As we laugh, cry, and pray together, not only are our friendships strengthened, but most importantly, our relationship with Jesus and our love for Him is deepened. The bottom line is we love Jesus more!

Read Galatians 6:1-2, 10. What do these verses say about accountability?

Christian friends can help you see, heed, and please God. Choosing accountability means opening yourself up to:
- questions and praise,
- vulnerability and nurturing,
- listening and speaking,
- correction and compliments.

Which of each pair is easier for you? Why?

But That's Personal!

Accountability gets downright personal. Accountability involves submitting to another. Submission is often met with suspicion. Invariably the word conjures up a picture of oppression. In contrast, the biblical meaning of submission is "a voluntary yielding in love, a readiness to renounce one's own will for the sake of others." Jesus Christ is the ultimate example of submission. He gave His life voluntarily. Not a wimpy action, submission shows true power and trust. Let your desire to serve Jesus totally be your motivation for submitting to the scrutiny of others. Let devotion to Him prompt you to become obedient.

A misunderstanding of submission is that it leaves us dependent. But the body of Christ is not characterized by dependence. Dependence keeps people from wholeness. Dependence means you are unable to function as an autonomous, free agent. Dependence is crippling. Independence is not the answer either. We're not loners, living out a private, eccentric, aloof Christian life. Independence produces proud, pretentious people.

Rather, God intends us to live in interrelatedness and affirmation. Interdependence produces whole, loving, serving people. It is the Body using each member's gifts for the sake of the whole. It is the Body cooperating together in love, to see men and women coming to Christian maturity in accountable, interdependent relationships (Eph. 4:13-15). When you're interdependent, you care enough about someone else to challenge him to a higher standard of Christian living. Accountability doesn't mean you seek to control or impose your expectations on him; instead, you challenge to respond to God's work in his life.

As you ponder submitting to a Christian who can help you grow in integrity, think about the questions you could ask one another. How could you voluntarily yield to one another in ways that would help you both live for Christ more authentically? My accountability group uses these questions:

1. **Have you spent daily time in Scriptures and prayer?**
2. **Have you had any flirtatious or lustful attitudes, tempting thoughts, or viewed or heard any explicit materials that would not glorify God?**
3. **Have you been completely above reproach in your financial dealings?**
4. **Have you spent quality relationship time with family and friends?**
5. **Have you done your 100 percent best in your job, school, etc.?**
6. **Have you told any half-truths, or outright lies, putting yourself in a better light to those around you?**
7. **Have you shared the Gospel with an unbeliever this week?**
8. **Have you taken care of your body through daily physical exercise and proper eating and sleeping habits?**
9. **Have you allowed any person or circumstance to rob you of your joy?**
10. **Have you lied on any of your answers today?**

Living our daily lives in such a way that pleases God should be the most important goal in life. When we live out integrity in the small issues, it is much easier to live it in the bigger issues.

What choices on your part would bring total accountability to a friend?
What attitudes are necessary for effective accountability?
What kind of spirit makes partners good accountability partners?

Our theme verse is:

"Therefore, brethren,

be all the more diligent

to make certain about

His calling and

choosing you;

for as long as you

practice these things,

you will never stumble"

(2 Pet. 1:10 NASB).

Encourage Your Group: Actions for Group Study

1. A quiet time can be defined as spending time alone with God and allowing Him to speak to you through His Word. Why is time alone with God the key to integrity?

2. Share one tip you've discovered on how to have an effective quiet time, such as the devotional guide(s) you use, the places you go, the way you stay focused.

3. God wants to be the hub of your wheel rather than an extra spoke in your life. How does God help you organize your time rather than add more pressure to it?

4. How can another person encourage you to develop a consistent quiet time?

5. Discuss the troubles Bible characters created by trying to go it alone, in the section "Integrity? What's the Big Deal?" Share a similar experience from your own life and how accountability might have prevented it. (CAUTION: Show compassion rather than try to top each others' stories.)

6. Explain the following reasons for accountability using absolutely no churchy words. Take turns monitoring presentations to insist on translating any theologizing. (The point: if you can explain without theological words, you truly understand.)
    - Satan's schemes
    - Holiness so the world can see Jesus
    - Personal relationship with Christ
    - God's judgment
    - Mutual encouragement

7. Tell why each member of these accountability pairs needs the other action:
    - questions needs praise, and praise needs questions;
    - vulnerability needs nurturing, and nurturing needs vulnerability;
    - listening needs speaking, and speaking needs listening;
    - correction needs compliments, and compliments need correction.

8. Create accountability questions that fit you. Feel free to use my group's questions as a model.

Between You and God

1. Is quiet time a spark that gets your devotion to God burning, or is it the only time you spend with Him? Why?

2. Name the place and time you'll have your quiet time for the next six weeks.

between you
and God

3. Who could motivate you to have your quiet time? How will you invite him or her to do this?

4. Review these reasons for accountability to discover the one that most powerfully motivates you to be held accountable:
   • Satan, our enemy, loves to see us stumble.
   • The world is closely watching us.
   • To remain right with the Lord.
   • Judgment is coming.
   • Accountability encourages us.

5. What temptations, time pressures, and demands do you face?

How might accountability to other Christians help you manage these?

6. "Two are better than one, because they have a good return for their work: If one falls down, his friend can help him up" (Eccl. 4:9-10). Do you believe this verse? Why?

7. What do you appreciate about submission?

Who models it well for you, besides Jesus?

8. Answer the ten accountability questions listed earlier, either alone or with
   a trusted Christian friend.

9. Complete the following sentences:
   When I consider my daily schedule, I know I need to . . .

The one thing I am going to focus on doing differently this next week is . . .

integrity

Why Do Friends and Family Matter?

Are your friendships draining or replenishing? Draining friendships take more from you than they give. You may enjoy the friends, but when they leave, you're spent. On the flip side, replenishing friendships leave you feeling cheerful, energized, and motivated. These friends strengthen and equip you to face life. You do the same for them. Develop relationships with at least as many replenishers as drainers, but let your closest relationships—your roommates, dates, friends—be replenishers. You need the mutual encouragement of positive Christian friendships. Hebrews 10:25 says it like this: "Let us not give up meeting together, as some are in the habit of doing, but let us encourage one another—and all the more as you see the Day approaching." Christian friends remind you how to follow God, and why following Him is pure delight.

This encouragement doesn't happen automatically. Deliberately seek out Christian friendships and nurture them. Take time to ask about their day, go places together, share a meal, and more. Bring light into others' lives. Cultivate the kind of togetherness the Bible calls fellowship (Acts 2:42 and 2 Cor. 6:14).

Friends and family are important because they are the ones with whom we travel through life. They are the ones who encourage us, teach us, cry with us, rejoice with us. Name a way by which you currently keep each of these relationships strong:

Parents:
Brother or sister:
Professor or mentor:
Pastor or other church leader:
Campus minister:
Roommate:
Close friends:
High school friends:
Dorm friends:
Boyfriend or girlfriend:

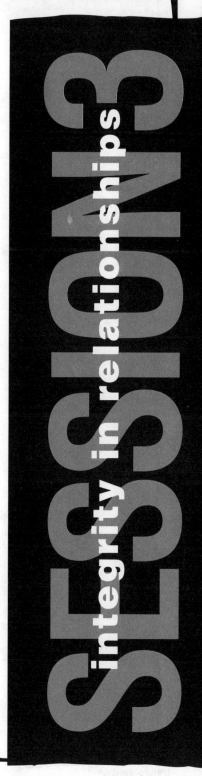

SESSION 3

integrity in relationships

What Do Friends and Family Have to Do with Integrity?

In friendships, integrity is a major issue. We may be tempted to use a generous person or neglect a forgiving person. We may use our personal influence to control people or make them feel belittled. Or we could respond to the generous person with even greater generosity. We could give greater attention to the forgiving person. We could use our personal influence to build up others and encourage them.

Maintaining healthy relationships isn't easy. Roommates, parents, professors, and boyfriends or girlfriends give us plenty of opportunity for conflict, resentment, deception, and outright dishonesty. Identify five phrases that describe relationships which have integrity.

1.
2.
3.
4.
5.

Have you ever taken advantage of a friend or family member rather than shown love toward them? What happened?

When have you let a family member or friend use you or otherwise sin against you?

Friendships with Integrity

God has given us friends for great reasons. They enrich our lives, keep us company, point us in the right direction, and can keep us spiritually sharp. Because we become like the people we hang out with, choose your friends well. At first you won't know friends well enough to tell the difference between strong and weak ones. But as you get to know people better, deliberately spend more time with those who prod you on to godliness. These people will be harder to find, but time with them is crucial. Paraphrase these verses to find out why:

Proverbs 13:20

Proverbs 27:17

1 Corinthians 15:33

Especially during college, the people you choose as friends help determine your life path. Because you go to school with them, live with them, eat every meal with them, and attend or avoid church with them, your friends have a huge impact on you, and you on them. Many students experience significant spiritual growth during college because of the friends they choose. Sadly, the opposite is also true. Many students end up spiritually dormant because of those they choose to hang out with.

What qualities, besides Christian commitment, does God want you to seek in friends?

We need to have both Christian and non-Christian friends. How can you strike a balance between the two?

A Model for Family Relationships

A relationship with your family can be difficult to maintain in college, especially if you attend a school far away from home. In addition, the relationship undergoes change. College begins a new stage in life, a transition into adulthood. Independence combined with busyness can create distance between you and your parents and siblings. It takes effort to write a letter, call, or email. A visit means changing your usual routine and maybe finding the money for travel. But because your family gave you roots and much more, it's important to keep that relationship strong.

How has your relationship with your family changed since entering college?

What makes you want to keep in touch with family?

What words have you not communicated lately with your family that need saying?

The book of Ruth tells about a family relationship that endured through hardships. The love and loyalty that led Ruth to stay with her mother-in-law can be a model for our relationships with family. Read Ruth 1-4, then reflect on these questions:

How did Ruth and Naomi become close?

Ruth and Naomi were from different lands and different families. When Naomi's son died, Naomi urged Ruth to return to her people and find another husband. Why did Ruth refuse?

How did the two women survive in this new place? What do you find most intriguing about their story?

How did Ruth demonstrate integrity and accountability to Naomi?

How did Naomi demonstrate integrity and accountability to Ruth?

The story of Ruth and Naomi had a happy ending. But loyalty to friends and family is valuable even without a happy ending. When could this be true?

Describe a relationship you are in that needs more loyalty. Name specific actions God wants you to do to demonstrate loyalty:

More Than Words

Read these passages and consider how following their commands demonstrates integrity to the people in our lives. Then answer the questions included.

John 13:34-35—How can you tell if someone genuinely loves you? What might initially look like love but actually be something different?

John 15:12-13—Give three examples of ways you have laid down your life for a friend, then three examples of ways friends have laid down their lives for you.

Romans 14:19—How can you tell the difference between working for peace and letting someone selfishly have his way?

1 Thessalonians 5:11—How is encouragement different from feeding an inflated ego? What good does encouragement bring to the receiver? to the giver?

More Than Closing Your Mouth

Part of being a good friend and a good family member is being a good listener. It's harder than it sounds. Here are a few tips for becoming a better listener:

1. Make eye contact. This communicates, "I'm available; I'm choosing to listen to you." Don't think about your schedule, assignments, or other people. Make a deliberate effort to truly hear your friend.
2. Ask questions, when needed, to encourage your friend to talk. There are times to be quiet and just listen, but many times your questions can help your friend see a new side, think through options, and make smart choices.
3. Avoid clock-watching. When you need to study or have another appointment, let the person know up front. Then set your watch to remind you both to stop. Keeping previous commitments is as important as listening. If you have unlimited time, refuse to look at your watch to give your complete attention.
4. Briefly mix in your experiences, if appropriate. Do not dominate the conversation, or try to top your friend's story. When needed, add your own thoughts without disrupting the flow of the conversation.

Live Out Your Accountability with Dates and Future Mates

I am pleased that purity is part of the CrossSeekers Covenant. Choosing to honor your body as the temple of God, dedicated to a lifestyle of purity is God's desire for you. As a youth you may have made a commitment to True Loves Waits. Let me encourage you to continue that commitment to purity as a collegian.

When I married, I was 32 years old and a virgin. I admit it wasn't easy to remain pure, but I did it! There were times of frustration and discontent wondering if God was going to bless me with a mate. At times while dating, my conduct was not at a level which pleased God or myself, but He protected me in a powerful way.

When dating, commit first to date only other Christians. The person you date may become not only your spouse, but a parent to your children. He or she will impact every day of the rest of your life. While you can't tell everything about a person's character and level of Christian commitment before you date, there are significant signs:
• Does this person attend church and campus fellowship activities regularly?
• Does this person treat all people kindly?
• Does this person have a self-confidence and sense of happiness with life?

Get to know the person in group situations first. Once you've seen hints of a person's character, try a date or two. Keep evaluating, and back off as soon as you see more differences than similarities. Once you know you wouldn't marry someone, it's never a good idea to keep dating him or her. If you're wrong, you can renew the friendship and resume dating later.

Young adults today are delaying marriage later than previous generations. Chances are you will remain single for several years after college as I did. The sexual temptations will only become stronger. We live in a society inundated with sex. Daily we are told that sex is normal, expected, and a sign of true love. Our own longings for love and our God-given passions push us toward physical expression of our feelings. But controlling that passion is the best way to keep it strong and growing, even when you want to marry the person.

God's Word tells us, "Do you not know that your body is a temple of the Holy Spirit, who is in you, whom you have received from God? You are not your own; you were bought at a price. Therefore honor God with your body" (1 Cor. 6:19-20). Honor God by staying pure until marriage.

Following are some pointers to help you stay focused as a single:

1. Be thankful for your singleness. It isn't a form of punishment from God. There are many benefits to being single.
2. Nurture your relationship with Christ. Focus on becoming the person God wants you to be rather than expending energy trying to catch a mate. Remember that no spouse can meet your every need. Only Christ can do this.
3. Build friendships with members of the opposite sex for the sake of friendship only. This allows you to meet people without applying pressure.
4. Be selective about what you read, watch, and listen. What you let yourself be exposed to will strongly affect your actions and attitude. Psalm 101:3 says, "I will set before my eyes no vile thing. The deeds of faithless men I hate; they will not cling to me."
5. Remember that sex is a wonderful gift from God, yet it is reserved solely for marriage. No matter how strong the temptation, wait until your wedding day. It is well worth the wait!
6. Trust Jesus. He is faithful and will provide the right person at the right time, if it is part of His plan. Remember, "No temptation has seized you except what is common to man. And God is faithful; he will not let you be tempted beyond what you can bear. But when you are tempted, he will also provide a way out so that you can stand up under it" (1 Cor. 10:13).

Read 1 Corinthians 6:12-20. This passage was written to the Corinthians, many of whom felt that what they did in the "flesh" wouldn't affect their spirit. What is meant by the phrase, "Everything is permissible. . .but not everything is beneficial"?

Verse 18 instructs us to "flee from sexual immorality." Why did God choose the word "flee"? Why not "walk away from" or "leave"?

Why does God want you to date only Christians with high character?

What excuses do we make for not following this guideline?

What advice from Proverbs 27:17 can you apply to your dating life?

How can someone you date make you a better or a worse person?

Even when dating only Christians of high character, maintaining sexual purity isn't easy. Read 1 Thessalonians 4:3-7, noting God's commands.

How does sexual purity honor God?

How does sexual purity honor ourselves and those with whom we are in a relationship?

Identify three ways we can demonstrate integrity through our sexual conduct:

     1.

     2.

     3

Choose a Life of Sexual Purity

In the book *Seven Promises of a Promise Keeper*, Jerry Kirk gives the following principles for a life of purity. While he wrote these for married men, the principles apply to anyone.

1. ***Past mistakes don't mean future failure!***

   The God who can redeem and bless every other area of our lives can also take control of our sexual being. Confession and forgiveness can cleanse. Even if this is the third or fourth time we're starting down this path—or even the tenth or one hundredth time—it's still worth the effort.

2. ***Sexual purity is as much a matter of the mind as it is of the body.***

   Paul's words in Romans 12:1-2 are the key . . . If our bodies are to be a living sacrifice to God, we must start by being "transformed by the renewing of your mind." Physical sexual sin is usually the result of allowing sinful thoughts to take root in our minds and hearts.

3. ***Practicing sexual purity is a process as well as a commitment.***

   Our commitment to sexual purity requires development over time. It must be cultivated like any other godly habit or it will not be there when temptation comes . . . We should walk with both a bedrock commitment to certain standards and a constant humble understanding that, but for the grace of God, we would not be able to stand firm.

4. ***Don't pretend your desires don't exist.***

   Denial does no more to produce healthy sexuality than hedonism. God created us as sexual beings, and our desires are normal. We need to channel them in productive, God-given directions.

5. ***No substitute exists for personal accountability with other godly men.***

   Secret sins have much more power and usually last much longer than those we acknowledge to our brothers. And together we can grow in our commitment to and practice of purity.

6. ***Understand the importance of sexual purity to our marriages, families, and heritage.***

   Our faithfulness gives strength to our wives. Their deepest needs include affection, communication, trust, security, and confidence in our fathering. All of those are undermined by sexual and emotional unfaithfulness.

7. ***Understand the importance of sexual purity to our Christian witness.***

   Nothing undermines our influence more than sexual failure. We must work on purity not only for our own well-being and joy, but also for the health of the church.

8. ***Understand the importance of sexual purity to our own sexual fulfillment within marriage.***

   When we experience sexual intimacy, in God's design, we are yoked to the other person in a unique way. The two become one spiritually and emotionally when they become "one flesh." Thus, a man brings to his marriage bed every woman with whom he has ever had intercourse. Each can affect his ability to wholeheartedly and singlemindedly love his wife and enjoy true intimacy with her.

Excerpt from *Seven Promises of a Promise Keeper*. Copyright 1994, Promise Keepers. Used by permission.

Encourage Your Group:
Actions for Group Study

1. As a group, discuss how your relationship with family has changed since you entered college.

2. Discuss ways you and your family have dealt with issues that have arisen as you transition into adulthood.

3. Review the list of relationship actions at the end of "Between You and God." What relationship actions are needed by both family and friends?

4. Read 1 Corinthians 13:1-13. This passage describes the qualities of God's perfect love. Identify what those qualities are.

1.	4.	7.
2.	5.	8.
3.	6.	9.
		10.

5. The relationship between Ruth and Boaz is often used as an example of one that honors God. Identify ways both acted with integrity:

6. Why is being a Christian of high integrity only the first of many qualities you need in friends? in dates?

7. Too often, we view sexual temptations as a game: How far can I go and still not have sex? Can I push myself further and further and still not go "all the way"? How will honoring your future mate and God give you a better game plan?

8. Review these verses: Matthew 5:28; 1 Corinthians 6:18; 2 Timothy 2:22; James 1:14-15. Create a list of ways group members can encourage one another to sexual purity.

Between You and God

1. Describe the kind of friend you are to others.

2. Name ten people you spend time with. Determine whether each relationship is draining or replenishing and what God wants you to do about it.

betweeen you and God

3. How does God want you to become accountable for your relationships—through an accountability group, an accountability partner, or another way?

4. What action will you take this week to strengthen your relationships with:
   Parent(s)?

   Sibling(s)?

   Grandparent(s)?

   Another family member?

5. Which of the following pulls you down in maintaining sexual purity: a girlfriend? a boyfriend? movies? music? the Internet? books or magazines?

What changes do you need to make?

6. Name someone who helps you be a better friend. How does he or she do this?

7. From the following relationship actions, choose three that God is prompting you to develop over the next six months:

- Listening skills
- Communicating more through email, letters, or phone calls
- Speaking encouraging words
- Keeping in touch with family
- Keeping in touch with friends I don't see regularly
- Including new people in my friendship circle• Finding a way to serve another person
- Showing friendship to a person who needs Christ
- Giving people more time
- Considering others' feelings
- Strengthening my personal integrity
- Balancing time with family, friends, myself.

What will you do to fulfill this commitment?

8. Complete the following sentences:

When I consider my relationships, I know I need to. . .

The one thing I am going to focus on doing differently this next week is. . .

integrity

Who's That in My Path?

We have an enemy on the path to integrity. His name is Satan (or the devil). We serve an awesome God who desires for us to live life to the fullest. He gives us not only Himself, but accountability partners to help us on this journey. Unfortunately, Satan will do anything he can to block us from living a Christ-centered life. We know about him, but most of us just don't take his power seriously enough. Satan is first identified in Genesis 3:1 as a serpent "more crafty than any of the wild animals." Satan distorts God's truth and leads people into sin. In Genesis 3:15, the serpent received punishment from God: "he will crush your head." Right then Satan's doom was guaranteed. But until that final moment, Satan is bent on destroying people. Stubborn, angry, devious, and evil, he works hard to take as many people down as possible.

Revelation 12:1-17 paints a picture of Satan's anger—he's ticked, and he takes it out on us: "That ancient serpent called the devil, or Satan, who leads the whole world astray. He was hurled to the earth, and his angels with him. . . When the dragon [Satan] saw that he had been hurled to the earth, he pursued the woman . . . the dragon was enraged at the woman and went off to make war against the rest of her offspring—those who obey God's commandments and hold to the testimony of Jesus" (vv. 9, 13, 17).

If Satan came as a red guy with a pitchfork, we'd all know to run. But instead, he comes as the father of lies (John 8:44). He distorts and twists the truth. He lies about God and His love for us. He will do anything to get us arguing with people or second-guessing ourselves. He entices us into doing the wrong thing, and worse, believing that we can get away with it. Satan is the opposite of God in every character quality. Regardless of his method, his goal is to deceive, destroy, rule, and accuse. He will do whatever is necessary to accomplish his goals. There is nothing good in him. Even so, he masquerades as an angel of light (2 Cor. 11:14). He makes wrong look right, and danger look fun. He waters down what really matters, so we'll settle for cheap imitations of God's best.

SESSION 4

integrity in school and work

Sometimes Satan is blunt—inviting people to openly worship him. More often he prowls silently and pounces before we realize he's even there. First Peter 5:8-9 says it like this: "Be self-controlled and alert. Your enemy the devil prowls around like a roaring lion looking for someone to devour. Resist him, standing firm in the faith, because you know that your brothers throughout the world are undergoing the same kind of sufferings."

Read John 8:44. What lies of Satan's have you swallowed? How did the hook hurt when you took it back out?

Read 2 Corinthians 11:14. When have you visited Satan's masquerade party? How did he deceive you?

Satan's strategy is well planned, but the Christian's weapons are more powerful. What weapons do we have against Satan? (See Eph. 6:10-18 for ideas.)

Isolation is one of Satan's most powerful tools. The banana pulled from the bunch is the one that gets peeled. FCA senior vice president Ralph Stewart uses a soccer illustration to warn us against this: "One tactic of an offensive-minded soccer team is to get a player isolated one-on-one against the goalie. At this point he has an excellent chance to score. Satan tries a similar attack on God's people. If he can get the Christian separated from the encouragement of fellow believers, the Christian is weakened." How can you make certain you don't isolate yourself, leaving you open to Satan's attacks?

I Don't Have Much to Do with Satan

Perhaps you feel safe because you don't dabble in satanic stuff. But two of Satan's prime turfs are school and work. He gets you thinking that God doesn't really care about that everyday stuff—that God is more interested in Sundays and church. Satan tries to segment your life so you separate worship from daily tasks. As a result, you end up slacking off at work or taking shortcuts at school. Which of these sins have you committed or been tempted to commit?

___ Let other students in a group project do most of the work.
___ Slack off when the boss isn't looking.
___ Call in sick when you're really not.
___ Sleep through class.
___ Buy a test, copy from another person, or otherwise take advantage of someone else's work.
___ Steal little stuff from work, like paper clips and pens, or use the copier without permission.
___ Do the least you can get by with at work.
___ Do the least you can get by with in a class.
___ Other _____

Living a life of integrity means giving our best effort in whatever we do. It means that we take the little actions as seriously as the big actions. It means that we see every minute as on opportunity to worship God, to bring glory to Him.

Your primary work right now is school work. When you do your best, you honor God. This does not mean you must make all *A's* or come home with the highest grade. It does mean you focus your attention on school work. It means you study when you're fresh, and chat when you're tired. It means you get enough rest during the week to concentrate well in class. It means you show up for class, turn in assignments on time, take good notes, add to discussion, show interest in succeeding, and work for learning as well as for good grades. Your motivation for this is not class standing or acceptance to grad school, but devotion to God.

But This Isn't a Real Job!

Second to school right now is the job that pays your expenses to be there. This job may not be in the field you are preparing for; in fact it may be a job you hope never to do again. Even so, there are ways to glorify God in it. Even if your present job is not your lifetime ambition, you can set worthwhile goals, reflecting a positive, Christlike attitude.

Many folks equate ambition with self-seeking and wealth-gaining. But true ambition goes much deeper. Define it well and right. Let this Bible passage help: "Make it your ambition to lead a quiet life, to mind your own business and to work with your hands, just as we told you, so that your daily life may win the respect of outsiders and so that you will not be dependent on anybody" (1 Thess. 4:11-12).

Describe true ambition:

What light does this description shed on the world's definition of ambition?

Define "a quiet life." How does a quiet life differ from a boring or colorless life?

Describe a time you "won the respect of outsiders" through something you did in your daily life:

Who Ya Tryin' to Impress?

Colossians 3:17 instructs, "And whatever you do, whether in word or deed, do it all in the name of the Lord Jesus, giving thanks to God the Father through him." Colossians 3:23-24 adds, "Whatever you do, work at it with all your heart, as working for the Lord, not for men, since you know that you will receive an inheritance from the Lord as a reward. It is the Lord Christ you are serving."

God expects our best effort in all of our endeavors. Whether in the classroom, in a study group, on the job, on the athletic field, with friends, or with family, we do our best for God's glory. God is our audience, not our classmates, employer, professor, coach, or parents. When we remember that He is the One we serve, our performance can be centered solely on Him.

Review Colossians 3:17. Think about the different actions that fill your day. How could you perform each of these tasks in the name of the Lord? How could you show God's goodness and demonstrate integrity in each action?

I Don't Have Time for That Right Now!

Each of us is given the same 24 hours a day. How we use our time depends on our priorities and goals. We make the hours count for what we think is important. I am an advocate of working smart, not just long. At the end of life you will probably never hear someone say, "I wish I had spent more time at the office." Therefore, the important commodity called time requires attention to details and a specific plan of action, or our time can quickly begin to slip away. It is also crucial that we not become workaholics or loafers. Either label would be inappropriate for someone who claims to be a believer.

Many Christian students want to do their best at school and work, but time gets away from them. Learning to effectively manage time is tough, but crucial to being able to give our best. We can't accomplish what we set out to do unless we choose to plan. In his book *Tyranny of the Urgent,* Charles Hummel tells that Jesus Christ managed and controlled His time while He was on earth. Though He was God, He was also human, and He experienced all of the pressures and strains a shortage of time brings. Yet at the end of His brief three years of ministry, John 17:4 says, "I have brought you glory on earth by completing the work you gave me to do." With so many unmet physical and spiritual needs around Him, He had peace because He knew He had finished the work God had given Him.

The key to Christ's success was that He received His daily instructions in quiet moments from the Father. Consistently, you see that nothing came in the way of His intimate time with God. If Jesus needed this time with God, how much more do you and I need to seek it out? Jesus, though His ministry could have easily extended another five to 50 years, knew God in a way where He experienced tremendous peace. Hummel says, "The path to freedom is continuing day by day to meditate on the Scriptures and gain our Lord's perspective."

How we choose to spend our time is important. The choices we make demonstrate both commitment to God and personal integrity. Learning to manage our time is crucial to giving our 100 percent best to whatever we undertake. If we are always behind on schoolwork, late for our jobs, late turning in assignments, and absent from meetings, we aren't giving 100 percent.

Often it is small actions that catch people's attention rather than large events. What can you and other Christian collegians do to build reputations marked by integrity?

How does committed study of God's Word and prayer defeat Satan's schemes? How does ethical work defeat Satan?

Hints for Managing Your Time

1. Learn to delegate. Find people who are skilled (or teach them) to perform needed tasks. We tend to cling to the jobs we do well. But others can do them equally well. When you give work away, acknowledge, praise, and thank others for their effort.

2. Control your time. Don't let strong-willed or weak-willed people dominate your schedule. You are in charge of your time. Ephesians 5:15-16 says, "Be very careful, then, how you live—not as unwise but as wise, making the most of every opportunity, because the days are evil. Therefore do not be foolish, but understand what the Lord's will is." A schedule will free you, not constrain you.

3. Don't be governed by every emergency. Set your priorities and goals. Constantly evaluate to make sure you are on track. As Matthew 6:33 recommends, "But seek first his kingdom and his righteousness, and all these things will be given to you as well." When you follow the schedule God helps you set, you'll find time for it all.

4. Determine when certain tasks should be performed based on when you are at your best. Some tasks are better performed at certain times and under certain conditions. Know your rhythms and be in touch with how to maximize your time under the appropriate conditions. Ecclesiastes 3:1-11 tells us there is a time for "everything under heaven."

5. Learn to say no to good things, so you can say yes to the best. Several good things will vie for your time—campus ministry, student government, intramural sports, and more. Know when to say yes and no to each. Psalm 130:5 says, "I wait for the Lord, my soul waits, and in His word I put my hope."

6. Budget time in advance. Put into your schedule nonnegotiables such as classes, study, and work responsibilities. Then identify days of rest, personal time with family, date nights, play days…even your quiet time. After these are scheduled, then you can drop other items into your schedule. Psalm 31:14-15a stresses, "But I trust in you, O Lord; I say, 'You are my God.' My times are in your hands…"

7. Make a list of all unfinished projects, and attempt to do the most difficult one first. A list gives you perspective. You can reward yourself with the easier projects when the harder projects are over. Make it your goal never to pick up something twice. Another helpful hint is to make sure that everything you have has a home. If you can't find a place for something, perhaps it is something you shouldn't keep.

8. Use a daily planner or calendar that works for you. Carry it with you, and maintain a simple, useable system.

9. Do an accounting of your current daily routine through monitoring your time. How do you currently spend your time? Through this exercise you will find out what things chew up your time.

Being Salt and Light

In choosing how to spend your time, don't leave out sharing your faith. Matthew 5:13-16 says, "You are the salt of the earth. But if the salt loses its saltiness, how can it be made salty again? It is no longer good for anything, except to be thrown out and trampled by men. You are the light of the world. A city on a hill cannot be hidden. Neither do people light a lamp and put it under a bowl. Instead they put it on its stand, and it gives light to everyone in the house. In the same way, let your light shine before men, that they may see your good deeds and praise your Father in heaven."

School and work may be where you spend most of your time. Those two places can be where you make a tremendous impact for Christ. If they know you are a Christian, classmates and co-workers will closely watch you. And in the words of one song, "You're the only Jesus that some people may ever see." First Peter 2:12 says it this way, "Live such good lives among the pagans that, though they accuse you of doing wrong, they may see your good deeds and glorify God on the day he visits us."

Sharing God's love means being willing to share our story. Consider the blind man in John 9. When questioned by the authorities as to what had happened to him, he did not know all the answers, but the one thing he did know was revealed in verse 25: "I was blind but now I see!" Like the blind man, we don't have to know all the answers, but we do need to prepare. Working on verbalizing our testimony is important. We should always be ready to tell what God has done for us! In your story:

1. In three to five minutes, share how you came to know Christ personally.

2. Identify the specific steps of salvation including: recognition of the need for Christ in your life, turning away from the sinfulness of your life, accepting Christ's forgiveness for your sins, and receiving Jesus Christ as Savior and Lord.

3. Use Scripture to illustrate these steps (Romans 3:23, Romans 6:23, Ephesians 2:8-9).

4. Cover the basics of the gospel including: our sinfulness which separates us from God; the life, teachings, death, and resurrection of Jesus Christ as the payment (atonement) for man's sins; and through faith in Jesus we are redeemed into "new life" as outlined in 1 Corinthians 15:1-4.

5. Tell of the changes Christ has brought into your life and what He means to you. Talk about things that will cause others to want to know Him as well. (Note: Be real, not pie in the sky. Include challenging and specific times of growth.)

6. Conclude with an illustration (if appropriate) to capture the theme of your testimony.

7. Tell how they can become a Christian by reviewing the meaning of salvation and presenting Scripture, and if appropriate, be ready to issue a call to commitment.

8. Close in prayer.

As you share, remember we are not responsible for the outcome. We are only responsible for sharing what Christ has done in our lives. As you study, work, and play, be ready to tell others!

Encourage Your Group: Actions for Group Study

1. Ask group members to choose a piece of armor from Ephesians 6:10-18 and give an example of how to use it to defeat Satan and maintain integrity.

2. Discuss: Are you more likely to get caught by Satan because you don't pay enough attention to his schemes, or because you deliberately toy with wrong?

3. Share ideas for finding prime time to study, complete group or individual projects, and write papers.

4. Christians frequently receive ridicule from the media and from non-Christians. What could be done to help dispel this ridicule?

5. How can Christians demonstrate their commitment to live a life that is above the ordinary?

6. Put a mark on the scale closest to where you are in these issues, and then invite the group to offer advice:

I am completely organized _____   Organization?
with my time and affairs.   What's that?

I do my very best at school. _____   As long as nothing else is going on, I study.

Even the most boring work _____   I make it through work
takes on meaning because   so I can get to real life.
I set ambitions for Christ's sake.

7. What one study or work change does God want in your life?

8. How does the admonition, "We are not responsible for the outcome of sharing our faith," take some of the pressure off?

9. Tell about times you shared your faith. How did the opportunity develop? How did you feel at the time? What did you learn from the experience?

10. As time permits, practice sharing your testimony using the guidelines under "Being Salt and Light."

Between You and God

1. Colossians 3:23 says, "Whatever you do, work at it with all your heart, as working for the Lord, not for men." What needs to change in your school or work habits to live out this verse?

2. How would commitment to excellence impact a non-Christian classmate or professor? Give examples.

3. Name three obstacles that keep you from doing your best:

How will you overcome each obstacle?

4. Reflect on Jesus' ministry on earth. It lasted three years, yet at the end, He was confident He had accomplished the Father's will. Your college years will last around four years. What do you want to accomplish in that time, beyond earning a degree?

5. List your current commitments and how much time each takes. Do changes need to be made? Map out the changes you will make.

6. If you've never done so, write out your personal testimony. Practice it on your own or with a friend.

7. Someone who can hold me accountable for how I use my time is:

8. Complete these sentences:

When I consider my school and work, I know I need to . . .

The one thing I am going to focus on doing differently this next week is . . .

integrity

Now You're Getting a Little Too Personal!

So, how wisely did you spend your money yesterday?
What foods did you choose to eat?
How did your thought life honor God?

Whoa! What does all this have to do with Christianity? All that stuff is private; it's my own business. Right? Wrong! Every move we make either honors or dishonors God. What we do with our money, how we care for ourselves physically, and what we think matters, even when no one else knows. These issues also directly impact what we do openly.

Money Is a Tool

Does God care about our finances? "He'd better," you may be thinking, "'cause tuition payment is due real soon!" Yes, God cares about our financial needs. But He also cares about what we do with the money He provides. Read the following thoughts about money. Are any of them yours?

___ My credit cards keep me going. "Charge it" takes care of everything.

___ I don't need to understand personal finances; God will provide for all my needs.

___ The more money I have, the happier I'll be.

___ What I earn is mine to spend. It's none of God's business.

___ I'll give back to God when I'm earning a big salary and have funds to spare.

___ I understand that my money is really God's, and I joyfully support His work with my finances.

SESSION 5

integrity in the hidden things

Christians have as many problems with money issues as non-Christians. Following are five Scripture truths concerning money. What does each tell us?

Proverbs 22:7

Proverbs 23:5

James 3:16

1 Timothy 6:10

Malachi 3:10

You may be thinking this section is a waste of time, since college is probably when finances are tightest. Think again. Good money management is tough, whether you are a struggling student or on a career track. The attitudes and practices you develop toward money now will follow you through the rest of your life. If you're not careful, the debt you accumulate can hang over your head for years to come and possibly for the rest of your life. According to Consolidated Credit Counseling, the average outstanding credit card balance for college students is $2,226, and only 34 percent of collegians understand the concept of buying on credit. How we use what God gives us shows good or poor stewardship.

A few suggestions to help you manage your finances:

1. Save small amounts regularly. It adds up to large sums over time.
2. Keep track of all expenditures (including cash) and review them at the end of each month so you know where your money goes.
3. Distinguish between wants and needs. Focus spending on the needs.
4. Pay off your credit card balance every month and use only credit cards with no annual fee.
5. Drop add-on services you can do without, such as caller ID on your telephone.
6. Consider your car a mode of transportation, not a status symbol.
7. Find and enjoy simple pleasures such as good conversation over coffee, touch football in the park, etc.

A Good Body Shows Integrity

Don't snicker! I'm not talking about a drop-dead figure or abs of steel, but a body that is well fed, rested, and maintained. God gives us only one body; therefore, we need to treat it properly. First Corinthians 6:19-20 warns, "Do you not know that your body is a temple of the Holy Spirit, who is in you, whom you have received from God? You are not your own; you were bought at a price. Therefore honor God with your body." We have a responsibility to properly care for what God has created.

Three keys to functioning well are sleeping, eating, and exercising. When we're rested, we can use our minds better. We can more readily recognize the truth and more deliberately live it. When we're sleepy, we're more emotional, less focused, and less efficient. We're apt to make mistakes or fail to think things through.

God has created each of us with a certain requirement for rest. Too little or too much sleep leaves us fatigued and compromises our decision making ability. Determine your optimum sleep pattern and then plan backwards. Fit your responsibilities into the remaining time. For example, if you have an 8:00 a.m. class and need eight hours of sleep, you'll go to bed at 11:00 p.m. and get up at 7:00 a.m. You get your homework done by 8:30 p.m. so you can go to campus-wide worship at 9:00 p.m. Because you chat extensively after supper, you'll be wise to finish your schoolwork by suppertime.

God has also created us with a requirement for exercise. Psalm 139 tells us how intricately we were made in the womb. Developed from 23 chromosomes from each parent, we become one specially formed person. We have 206 bones, muscles, joints, ligaments, and tendons making up an active body. So find a way to keep that fearfully and wonderfully made body wonderful instead of fearful.

A third requirement to maintaining our bodies is adequate fuel. A car running on empty eventually stops. So it is with our bodies. The kind of food we eat is just as important as how much we eat. We've studied nutrition charts since elementary school. Now is the time to make smart choices and put that knowledge into practice.

Rate these sleep obstacles from 1 to 6 with 6 being death to sleep for you:
___ Talking to friends
___ Procrastinating on schoolwork
___ Jay, David, or Conan
___ Partying
___ Weekday dates
___ OTHER: _____

Rate these exercise obstacles from 1 to 6 with 6 being, "I never exercise because of this":
___ I'm too busy.
___ I hate to exercise.
___ Nobody knows whether I exercise or not.
___ It's too hot (or cold, or rainy, or ...).
___ I'm self-conscious about my performance in sports.
___ OTHER: _____

Rate these food traps from 1 to 6 with 6 being, "I destroy my body regularly with this":
___ Eating junk food
___ Eating on the run
___ Fad diets
___ Not eating
___ Eating too much
___ OTHER: _____

What body battle is toughest for you: exercising, getting adequate rest, or eating properly?

How is God guiding you to master this area?

Alcohol and Drugs:
Temptations with a Hook

One huge temptation for many college students is the use of drugs and alcohol. On your own for the first time, you may decide a little won't hurt. You may reason you deserve a little fun. Never mind that this is a lie. Never mind that this lie will take away your fun, and possibly your life. Never mind that alcohol and drugs actually depress and destroy your body.

Deciding whether to use drugs and alcohol will be a major temptation in college, if you haven't already faced it in high school. Alcoholic beverage companies target college age students in hopes you'll be hooked into drinking for life. The messages are incessant: drinking makes you cooler, smarter, more fun, more popular.

As you struggle with this issue, consider the following:

1. Don't use when prohibited by law. If a drug is illegal, or if you are under legal drinking age, it's a no-brainer. Don't.

2. Consider your impact. Something may not seem wrong to you, but it may be a serious stumbling block to someone else. Consider the following Scriptures:
   - "And if anyone causes one of these little ones who believe in me to sin, it would be better for him to be thrown into the sea with a large millstone tied around his neck" (Mark 9:42).
   - "So I strive always to keep my conscience clear before God and man" (Acts 24:16).
   - "So then, each of us will give an account of himself to God. Therefore let us stop passing judgment on one another. Instead, make up your mind not to put any stumbling block or obstacle in your brother's way" (Romans 14:12-13).
   - "Everything is permissible"—but not everything is beneficial. "Everything is permissible"—but not everything is constructive. Nobody should seek his own good, but the good of others" (1 Cor. 10:23-24).

While you can find Bible folks who drank alcohol, you also find others like Daniel and John the Baptist who chose never to drink alcohol. This was a leadership move.

3. Be honest with yourself. Why do you want to drink? To have "fun"? To prove something? Because you never could before? Because you assume you're immune from its dangers? Don't kid yourself into thinking it's just a beverage. A commitment to abstinence opens up opportunities to tell others about Christ and eliminates many of the negative consequences.

I vividly remember being invited to a party within the first week of my freshman year at college. As I entered the dorm, several of my football teammates hollered at me and rushed over with a beer for me. I refused the drink and stuck to my convictions the rest of the night. It was my goal to enjoy the party and show my friends true fun without alcohol. While maintaining friendships with my friends/teammates, they knew to provide a Dr. Pepper® when I showed up at the parties. Not drinking gave me a tremendous opportunity to share my faith. Even today, I've never had a sip of alcohol, and I've not missed out on anything.

How big a problem is alcohol and drug abuse on your campus?

What can Christian students do to impact this problem?

It's All in Your Head

Using drugs and alcohol will rob you of your joy. Have you also allowed any person or circumstance to rob you of your joy? Former FCA staff member Van Normand recommended this question to my accountability group. There is a distinct difference between joy and happiness. It has been said that happiness happens because of our circumstances, while joy happens in spite of our circumstances. Joy can also be described as "feeling contentment and peace inside because God's in charge outside." Joy isn't based on emotional feelings or events. It is a deep, ongoing certainty and sense of peace that no matter how rotten life is, God's still in control through every situation. Though our self image may take a beating, real joy is knowing God loves us deeply and unconditionally.

Happiness is often based on external circumstances or temporary situations. How you react to these situations can have tremendous impact on not only your spirit but also the spirit and attitude of those around you. There is no question that the day-to-day grind of life is difficult. In John 16:33 Jesus reminds us that in the world we will experience trouble. There will be tribulation, but we are not merely to endure it but to "be of good cheer" for He has overcome the world.

Being "successful" in the eyes of the world doesn't necessarily mean we will experience joy. Many in the world have attained riches, power, fame, and popularity, yet are miserable. They have achieved their success but have paid the high costs of losing family, friends, and even their own souls. Steve Largent, NFL Hall of Famer, warns about climbing the ladder of success but discovering at the top rung that the ladder had been leaning against the wrong structure. True success is walking in obedience with God, meditating on His Word, day and night (Joshua 1:7-8). FCA president Dal Shealy admonishes, "It's your attitude, not your aptitude, that allows you to get to a higher altitude, if you have enough intestinal fortitude."

As a college student, I, like many students, struggled with what God wanted me to do. I was frustrated and wanted to see down the road what was in store for me if I followed God with all my heart. A trusted friend pointed out, "The Bible says God's Word is a lamp unto your feet and a light unto your path, not a set of street-lights to the end of the road." Once I took one step, God's lamp would show me the next. Recognizing this truth enabled me to live it. Living it gave me the joy and peace I longed for. What we choose to do starts in our heads. Choosing to think about the truth ends up producing joy. Choosing to believe lies steals our joy.

Read Psalm 119:1-8. What does this passage tell us about experiencing joy?

Why would a question about letting others rob us of our joy be included in a list of accountability questions?

Your Head Becomes Clearer with Accountability

Choosing accountability may sound like walking into a prison and giving someone else the key. But accountability is actually freeing. It gives you benefits you find no other way. Accountability brings:

1. Growth in Your Christian Walk.

You will be challenged and encouraged in a multitude of ways to trust God with your whole heart (Jer. 29:11-13). Knowing you don't face the battles of daily life and spiritual growth alone will strengthen you powerfully. Dietrich Bonhoeffer said, "Many people are looking for an ear that will listen…they do not find it among Christians, because these Christians are talking where they should be listening…one who cannot listen long and patiently will presently be talking beside the point and be never really speaking to others." To find people who will listen long and patiently is like discovering a treasure.

2. Deepening Friendships.

Not only will the depth of friendships increase in your group, but you will also find it easier to develop solid, meaningful friendships outside the group. Your friendships within the group will show you how to initiate conversations beyond normal surface issues. As you feel love and acceptance from your group, you find freedom to be yourself in other friendships.

3. Greater Awareness.

Because you will discuss real issues, your eyes will open to the needs and situations of everyday life. These issues include family, church involvement, integrity, half-truths, and a variety of other concerns. The simple act of sharing the raw material of daily life with an accountability group helps you see these through the eyes of others. James Houston of Regent College says, "Sin always tends to make us blind to our own faults. We need a friend to stop us from deceiving ourselves that what we are doing is not so bad. We need a friend to help us overcome low self-image, inflated self-importance, selfishness, pride, our deceitful nature, our dangerous fantasies, and so much else."

4. Priority Setting.

When our hectic schedules crowd out time for family relationships, friendships, prayer, or exercise, we need people to remind us that the tasks that seem so urgent are not worth the compromise.

5. Peace.

How would you feel if Christ returned and found you in the midst of a compromising or embarrassing situation? Accountability partners help you avoid this. Each time you encounter a situation which may not be appropriate, recall the words, "And now, dear children, continue in him, so that when he appears we may be confident and unashamed before him at his coming" (1 John 2:28).

6. A Support System.

Mammoth redwood trees hundreds of feet high and several feet thick grow in the Sequoia National Park in California. Most trees of this size have a root system equal to what you see above the surface. Not redwoods. They survive the storms and wind because they grow next to other redwoods. By binding together with one another, their root systems become incredibly strong. Because of their mutual support, they do not topple. Being in an accountability group will provide this type of support system.

How would you convince someone that these six advantages make it worth choosing accountability? Pretend this person is extremely resistant.

Reasons People Refuse Accountability

1. I'm the only one who struggles.
2. If they knew the truth about me, I would be rejected.
3. I can handle this on my own.
4. I've got too many problems to have someone carry those with me. No one really cares.
5. I've been burned in the past.
6. I'm too busy.
7. Hey, I'm okay. Accountability is for "really" sick people.
8. What I do privately is my own business.
9. I like the sin I'm wallowing in, and I don't want to get right and change my sin patterns.
10. I can't show any weaknesses. Too many people are counting on me.

Choose to Deliberately Please God

Choose to please God in all of life. By managing the "hidden things" in life well, you provide a public witness that is unspeakably powerful. You impact those around you with the power of God Himself. Through accountability, we can help each other be more like Christ, grow in these hidden things, avoid sin, and live a life of integrity. Then at the end of our lives we can hear Christ say, "Well done, good and faithful servant!" (Matt. 25:23).

Encourage Your Group: Actions for Group Study

1. In this session you have examined integrity in areas of your life that are not as visible as others. What other "hidden things" in our lives reflect our integrity?

2. Why is what you choose to believe an even more powerful issue than what you think about?

3. When have you allowed your joy to be robbed by choosing to believe a lie? (Examples: If I just had a boyfriend, I'd be happy; As soon as I get out of my parents' house I can do whatever I want; Nobody likes me.)

4. When have you found joy by choosing to believe a truth? (Examples: The happier I let God make me, the more attractive I'll be to girls; Some people like me and some don't, but God will always give me friends.)

5. Add ten more money management tips to the ones listed under "Money Is a Tool."

6. Review the six benefits of accountability under "Your Head Becomes Clearer with Accountability." What other benefits can you think of?

7. We become defensive when people point out inconsistent behaviors in some hidden things. What advice does Proverbs 27:6 offer?

8. How can you tell if stinging words are good advice or are meant to hurt?

9. Living for Christ is the most dynamic, exciting, and fulfilling journey you'll ever experience. How could you explain Christian joy to a non-believer?

Between You and God

1. Answer these accountability questions:
   • Have you been completely above reproach in your financial dealings?
   • Have you taken care of your body through daily physical exercise and proper eating and sleeping habits?
   • Have you allowed any person or circumstance to rob you of your joy?

2. If your answer to any of the statements in question one was no, what do you plan to do about it?

3. Recall a time you acted on truth, and joy followed.

4. Review Proverbs 22:7, Proverbs 24:3, James 3:16, 1 Timothy 6:10, and Malachi 3:10. How can these verses help you get money problems under control?

5. If you drink alcoholic beverages, list reasons you do. Then list what you gain by doing so. If you don't drink, ask these questions of someone who does.

6. Respond to this: Drs. Les and Leslie Parrott, in their book *Relationships,* say: "If you want to relate to God without feeling phony, you've got to get rid of everything that distorts, dilutes, or compromises the person you were meant to be, until only your authentic self—created in God's image—remains. The bottom line? You've got to take off any sanctimonious mask you may be wearing and be angry, depressed, excited, or anything else you consider 'bad' before God. The more you can admit who you are—even when you wish you were different—the deeper your relationship with God will grow."

7. The key to accountability is to determine areas of your life where you need immediate and specific help. What are these areas for you?

8. Choosing to see and abide by truth is the most powerful witness you can give others. Why does this show God's power? What else does it show about God?

between you and God

9. Complete the following sentences:

When I consider areas of my life known only by God and me, I know I need to . . .

The one thing I am going to focus on doing differently this next week is . . .

integrity

Just a Fad Idea?

An accountability group—a small group of believers who prompts you to obey God in every area of life—is more than a fad sweeping college campuses. The accountability group is a concept that has stood the test of time. John Wesley developed an accountability model in the mid-1700's. He influenced thousands of people into Christian discipleship and growth. Wesley said, "Preaching like an apostle without joining together those that are awakened and training them in the way of God is only begetting children for the murderer."

Wesley organized his converts and leaders in small cell groups for mutual care and discipleship. Following are guidelines he established for these groups. These guidelines were to be followed in the spirit of the law, not the letter of the law:

It is agreed by us:
1. That we will meet together once a week to confess our faults one to another, and pray one for another that we may be healed.
2. To come punctually at the hour appointed without some extraordinary reason.
3. To begin, (those of us present), exactly at the hour with singing and prayer.
4. To speak each of us in order, freely and plainly, the true state of our souls, with the faults we have committed in thought, word, or deed, and the temptations we have felt since our last meeting.

Following are some questions people were asked before being admitted to the cell groups:
1. Have you peace with God through our Lord Jesus Christ?
2. Have you the forgiveness of your sins?
3. Has no sin, inward or outward, dominion over you?
4. Do you desire to be told of your faults?
5. Do you desire to be told from time to time whatever is in our heart concerning you?
6. Consider! Do you desire that we should tell you whatsoever we think,

SESSION 6

integrity through accountability groups

7. Do you desire in doing this that we should come as close as possible, that we should cut to the quick and search your heart to the bottom?

8. Is it your desire and design to be on this, and all other occasions, entirely open so as to speak everything that is in your heart without exception, without disguise and without reserve?

The following five questions were asked at every meeting:

1. What sins have you committed since our last meeting?

2. What temptations have you met with?

3. How were you delivered?

4. What have you thought, said, or done of which you have doubt whether it be sin or not?

5. Have you nothing you desire to keep secret?

Wesley believed that every member should be responsible for every other member. They sought to share with each other a lifestyle of openness, transparency, a caring community, and submission.

True Characters

"The measure of a man's real character is what he would do if he knew he would never be found out."
—Thomas B. Macaulay

"A man of integrity is secure. The one who lacks integrity will be exposed. We may hide our lack of integrity for a while, but never from God, and never for long."
—Jeff Comment

"Accountability is the greatest prize of integrity. Accountability starts with yours truly—with an honest appraisal of who we are, of what makes us tick. It includes a long, hard look at our own ideas and motives. When we give an accurate account of what we think and what we do, then those around us can come to rely on us with confidence."
—Ted Engstrom

What Does The Bible Say About Accountability?

While the phrase "accountability group" isn't used in the Bible, the Bible says much about believers helping each other. The verses stress mutuality—helping others, but not to the extent that our own responsibilities are compromised. At the same time, we take care of our own responsibilities, but not to the extent of selfishness or isolation.

Find the two-part command about burdens in Galatians 6:1-5. Summarize it here:

Describe a time you've done too much of the 6:2 part:

Describe a time you've done too much of the 6:5 part:

What other dangers are cited in Galatians 6:1-5?

How could an accountability group help you with these dangers?

What's the difference between restoring someone gently and restoring him in a sanctimonious or harsh way?

How Do We Start?

Your group has discussed many integrity issues these past five sessions. You've looked at your commitment to God and how accountability can help live that out. You've discovered ways to let Jesus become the center of your life. You've explored how to choose and develop positive relationships in your life. You've met your nemesis the devil and examined ways to defeat him. You've discovered how personal excellence honors God and ways you can live out that excellence at school and work. You've discussed what integrity means in your private and public worlds. You've examined character in each area of your life.

An excellent way to put all of this together is to begin an accountability group. Here are nine steps to getting started. Jot next to each your thoughts and questions. Then plan to talk these over with your group.

1. Pray and risk.

Talk to God about forming an accountability group. Ask Him to guide you to the right person(s). Don't get frustrated if God takes time to reveal His person(s) to you. Supportive relationships where you discuss your weaknesses and failures are risky. Pray for God to show you people who also desire to have a committed relationship to Jesus Christ and others. Ephesians 1:17 says, "I keep asking that the God of our Lord Jesus Christ, the glorious Father, may give you the Spirit of wisdom and revelation, so that you may know him better."

accountability

2. Initially find at least one person to whom you are willing to be accountable.

In the working world everyone is accountable to someone. Even the self-employed are accountable to customers and clients. Successful businesses challenge their employees to perform certain tasks. The employee then has opportunity to run with the goals and make things happen. With that freedom comes the challenge for accurate reporting and a completed project. This is accountability.

It's similar in our personal lives. Without challenge, opportunity, and reporting, we, like sheep, will go astray (Isa. 53:6). So establish that process by finding at least one person to hold you accountable.

Finding one or more accountability partners is not easy. The overriding qualities are love for Christ, personal wholeness, desire to see you succeed, and recognition of the need for accountability in their own lives. Pick people whom you respect, with whom you feel compatibility, and whose judgment you trust. Otherwise you second-guess the person asking you the hard questions. Proverbs 13:20 says, "He who walks with the wise grows wise, but a companion of fools suffers harm."

3. Decide the key areas for accountability.

Every group must determine the areas where accountability is needed. Members discuss areas in which they need consistency and then together design a set of questions to ask each other weekly (see Wesley's list and my list in session two for examples). They also challenge each other in areas that come up fresh each week.

To better understand accountability groups, consider the way icebergs work. An iceberg is one of nature's most beautiful and dangerous phenomena. What shows above the surface is beautiful. This obvious part is like the "best foot" each of us puts forward with our friends. But these broken-off glaciers show only one-eighth to one-tenth of themselves. The rest is hidden below the surface of the water. That is where the danger lurks. The magnificent British steamer, the *Titanic,* was considered by experts to be unsinkable. But when the *Titanic* struck the hidden part of an iceberg on its maiden voyage the night of April 14, 1912, one of the largest sea disasters in history occurred. This has two implications. First, don't enter into accountability with someone you've known only a short time. Second, choose partners who will look beneath your surface with both compassion and commitment.

Like an iceberg, our lives have areas that others can see and parts that they cannot. What's below the surface is where we live our real lives. These lives are too often hidden from the scrutiny of other Christians. The jagged subsurface edges of our secret lives rip open our relationships and damage our spiritual lives. Or they build and strengthen those relationships. Accountability helps the latter happen. Let accountability examine what is unseen so it won't sink you. Accountability brings these issues to the surface where they can do no harm.

The Accountability Iceberg

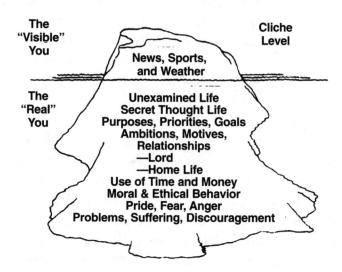

The
"Visible"
You

Cliche
Level

News, Sports,
and Weather

The
"Real"
You

Unexamined Life
Secret Thought Life
Purposes, Priorities, Goals
Ambitions, Motives,
Relationships
—Lord
—Home Life
Use of Time and Money
Moral & Ethical Behavior
Pride, Fear, Anger
Problems, Suffering, Discouragement

This drawing[1] illustrates that most conversation revolves around the cliché level of news, sports, and weather. This tip of the iceberg is all we show to most people; it's the "visible" you. The "real" you wrestles with gut-wrenching issues and important dreams that you long to share. Some of these are positive. Others are dangerous. Accountability gives you the freedom to navigate safely around the submerged dangers of an unexamined life. The key areas in which most all of us need accountability include: relationship with God, relationships with friends and dating partners, use of money and time, moral and ethical behavior, and areas of personal struggle.

4. Set a regular time and place, including a systematic method for getting through the questions.

Contact your accountability partner(s) frequently. I suggest a weekly meeting, although a bi-monthly one can also work. Too much happens in a month to meet less often than every two weeks. These guidelines can help:

a. Begin on time.

b. Limit general talk to a couple of minutes.

c. Have from two to five people in your group.

d. Let a different person begin each question, and juggle the order of the questions to meet needs.

e. Find your group's rhythm.

f. Limit your comments until each person has had the chance to respond.

g. Keep a running list of prayer requests and commitments people make.

h. Seek out the Word of God to discover biblical insights.

i. Share victories as well as defeats—don't focus exclusively on one or the other.

j. Close in prayer.

accountability

5. Establish a covenant.

This can seem a bit awkward, but it will give you a road map, a set of ground rules, structure, and boundaries. Most people come to a group with an assumed covenant, but unless those expectations are discussed openly, group members are seldom on the same page. So speak your covenant orally, write it down, and give every member a copy. The next section offers a sample covenant.

6. Be transparent.

You become a detriment to your accountability group if you are not honest. God has forgiven your sins, but experience teaches that secret sins are seldom overcome. When you confess to another person, sin often withers and dies. Sin flourishes in the dark but withers in the light of Jesus Christ. So stop lying to yourself and to others. Dostoevsky's novel *The Brothers Karamazov* says, "The man who lies to himself and listens to his own lie comes to such a pass that he cannot distinguish the truth within him, or around him, and so loses all respect for himself and for others. And having no respect he ceases to love. . . ."

7. Stay on course.

Set clear, concise, and measurable goals. Then sail for them together. In an article in the February 16, 1997, *Kansas City Star,* Dr. Laura Schlessinger describes it like this: "Living for yourself and believing you're accountable only to yourself enables you to make and break the rules at whim."

8. Remember confidentiality is critical.

Accountability can be successful only when members cherish and trust each other. When truly cherished, each person can be totally honest, share struggles and successes, cry, enjoy, and confide in each other. For this loving environment to exist, each member must provide safety for the others. If members think information might leak from the group or a member might ridicule them, complete honesty is unlikely. As a group, you must covenant together that information shared in the group will remain in the group.

9. Chose celebration as well as chastising.

Accountability is not just for checking weaknesses. It is also for noticing strengths and building upon those. If members move toward sharing only weaknesses or strengths, prod them to share a little of both. We all have rootedness and dry rot. Notice and help each other with both. Along a similar line, get together at least occasionally for simple fun and fellowship. Share a meal. Play putt-putt golf. Just have fun together.

What would happen if one person in an accountability group chose to use information against someone?

celebration and chastising

How can you make certain you do not covenant with a person who will do this?

How can you recognize what someone is really like, rather than see what you want him to be?

What Covenant Shall We Make?

An accountability group is a covenant group. Like in a marriage, it's wise to take vows together. Write next to each covenant a reason it's crucial:

The Covenant   The Reasons

1. The Covenant of Affirmation (Unconditional Love):
   I may not agree with your actions, but I will love you for
   what Christ wants to make of you (1 John 4:7-12).

2. The Covenant of Availability:
   I pledge energy, wisdom, and time to you. As part of
   being available, I pledge regular time both in prayer
   and in meeting (Heb. 10:25).

3. The Covenant of Prayer:
   I promise to pray for you, uphold you, and attempt
   to listen to the Holy Spirit concerning your needs so
   that I can share them with you (Jas. 5:13-16).

4. The Covenant of Openness:
   I will strive to be open and transparent. I affirm you
   as a person I can trust (2 Cor. 6:11-13).

5. The Covenant of Sensitivity:
   Even as I desire to be known and understood
   by you, I covenant to be sensitive to you and
   your needs (Gal. 6:2, 10).

6. The Covenant of Honesty:
   I will trust our relationship enough to risk honesty,
   because in "speaking the truth in love" we
   grow up in every way (Eph. 4:15-16).

7. The Covenant of Confidentiality:
   What goes on in this group stays here. I will say
   nothing that could injure or embarrass you (1 Cor. 1:10).

8. The Covenant of Accountability:

You have the right to expect my growth in Christ.
You may ask me about goals I set with God,
my family, and my world. I expect you
to lovingly not "let me off the hook" (Prov. 27:17).

9. The Covenant of Friendship:

I will develop friendship with you (Prov. 18:24).

10. The Covenant of Nurture:

I will deliberately nurture an authentic interest in
you (Phil. 2:3-4).

11. The Covenant of Patience:

There is no such thing as an "instant accountability
group." I will not quit before the group has time
to develop (1 Cor. 13:4-5).

12. The Covenant of Equality:

We will treat others as equals. Each gift and
experience is valid. There are no "leaders" in
an accountability group (Gal. 3:28).

13. The Covenant of Listening:

I will hear you (Prov. 18:2, 19:27).

14. The Covenant of Unanswered Questions:

When we don't know the answer or solution
we will say so. We will pray and care (Phil. 4:6-7).

15. The Covenant of Encouragement

I will uplift and encourage you by believing
in you (1 Thess. 5:11).

Accountability plays a very important role in our Christian growth. I have grown so much over the past few years by being answerable to people in areas of my public, personal, and private life. I encourage you to seek out others who share your desire to also be accountable. I pray you will be blessed as I have been.

No two accountability groups will be identical, because every person brings unique skills and talents, a different background, and a different maturity level. Utilize the concepts and questions in this book to develop a model which will ultimately bring you closer to Jesus Christ. God bless you!

Encourage Your Group: Actions for Group Study

1. Divide your group in two and debate the pros and cons of accountability.

2. Accountability is a central tenant of CrossSeekers. Partnering with one or more Christians can become a way to live out the points of the CrossSeekers Covenant. Discuss how accountability could make these covenants come true:
   - I will be a person of integrity.
   - I will pursue consistent spiritual growth.
   - I will speak and live a relevant, authentic, and consistent witness.
   - I will seek opportunities to serve in Christ's name.
   - I will honor my body as the temple of God, dedicated to a lifestyle of purity.
   - I will be godly in all things, Christlike in all relationships.

3. Each of you choose one of the nine steps to starting an accountability group and explain how it would work on your campus and with your group.

When You Choose Accountability, Expect:

1. Growth in your Christian walk.
2. Deepening friendships.
3. Greater awareness of what's true and real.
4. Priority setting.
5. Peace.
6. Support system.

4. Pretend this study group is your accountability group. Write your own covenant, using ideas from "What Covenant Shall We Make?"

5. How can an accountability group maintain balance in the following areas, as guided by Galatians 6:1-5, Philippians 2:4, and Luke 6:41?
• Taking care of your own needs while helping others with theirs.

• Addressing successes as well as failures.

• Looking at the present as well as the past.

6. Recall a time you were hurt by an "iceberg person," someone who looked fine on the surface but was destructive underneath. How can you keep this from happening in your accountability group?

7. Develop a plan for starting an accountability group, putting together all you've discussed in session 6.

8. Review the list of accountability questions you developed in session 2. Do any questions need to be changed now? What questions would you add to or subtract from your list?

Between You and God

1. Accountability helps you become a person of integrity. Review the ten accountability questions under "But That's Personal!" in session two. In what areas of your life do you most want accountability?

2. Describe a friend who lives the balanced life as described in Galatians 6:1-5 and Philippians 2:4.

How well could the two of you be accountable to each other?

3. What characteristics should an accountability partner or group member possess?

4. Review the reasons you wrote for each covenant under "What Covenant Shall We Make?" Then write your own covenant of accountability that you'd want to keep in a group.

5. Jot down the name of one or more like-minded believers who might form an accountability group with you. Prayerfully consider what God may be leading you to do.

6. Complete the following sentences:

When I consider accountability in my life, I know I need to . . .

The one thing I am going to focus on doing differently this next week is . . .

Notes

1 Patrick M. Morley, *A Man in the Mirror*, (Nashville, TN: Thomas Nelson Publishers, 1992) 276-277.

leader's guide

transparentliving

living a life of integrity

Transparent Living: Living a Life of Integrity is a six-week study based on Rod Handley's book *Character Counts—Who's Counting Yours?* A delightfully challenging book, *Character Counts* offers specific strategies for living the Christian life God has called you to live.

Introduction to this Study

This study explores the following questions:
• Why should I care about integrity and character?
• Why do I need accountability—other people to help me stay on the right track?
• How can we Christians encourage each other to do right without sounding judgmental, condescending, or parental?
• What areas am I strong and weak in people skills, school focus, money use, work commitment, and caring for my body?
• What people will I call on to help me grow in Christian maturity?
• How can I find the time I need both to manage my life and grow in Christ?
• How can I let God become the center of my life?
• Do I lie to others and myself? How will I come clean?
• What people do I neglect, and how can I give them the attention they deserve?
• How do I build replenishing friendships, rather than draining ones?
• Am I honorable in my dating? in friendships? with family?
• How can I become pure, rather than diluted?
• How can I know what God wants me to do?
• What is an accountability group, and how can I establish one?

Group Study Leader Qualifications

Be curious—Desire to know God and how to live for Him.

Be interested—Show the people in your study group that you care about the details of their daily lives.

Be constant—Lead each of the six sessions by showing a caring spirit and by starting and ending on time.

Be in contact—with God, with His Word, with the people in your group.

Be watchful—Notice when God is teaching you and your group members. Don't miss His lessons.

Be responsive—Answer God's call to make new insights a part of your daily walk.

Be happy—Use humor, joy, enthusiasm, and your spiritual gifts. Make it easy for each group member to do the same.

Be un-preachy—We're making this a word to remind you not to lecture and preach. Instead, guide your group members to share life and learn with each other.

Guidelines for Effective Group Study Time

1. Choose six weeks that allow the greatest participation. Sometimes this means starting the week collegians arrive on campus, before they've had time to get involved in many activities. Other times it means getting the group together later, after the semester or quarter is underway.

2. Start on time. This encourages the whole group to be on time.

3. End on time. This lets busy collegians know they can get right back to finishing that school paper or studying for that test.

4. Allow 60 to 90 minutes for each session.

5. Challenge your group to read and complete that session's content before coming together to discuss it.

6. During the session, keep the discussion centered on the study. Jot stray subjects on paper. See number 8 "Issue Bin" under "During the Session."

7. Covenant together that all things shared in the group are to be kept ABSOLUTELY CONFIDENTIAL. . .TOP SECRET. . .CLASSIFIED. What's said in the group stays in the group. Only with trust and respect can openness and transparency happen.

8. Encourage all to share. Everyone-shares-one-sentence and similar safe-sharing strategies allow all to participate without making any feel overly vulnerable.

9. Encourage all members to bring their own Bibles so they can mark them as they make discoveries during a session.

During the Session

1. Your job is to facilitate the discussion. With key questions and purposeful waiting, get everyone involved and keep the discussion flowing. Questions throughout the sessions and under "Encourage Your Group" in each session will help with this process.

2. Open each session with prayer. Vary the ways you do this. Sometimes you or a group

member can pray a line or two. Other times, ask a group member to write requests while others share them. Then close this open-eyed prayer with an "amen."

3. Introduce a no-slam rule. Insist that group members never put down another's comment, idea, or concern. Instead, prompt the active encouragement detailed in Hebrews 10:24-25.

4. Be sensitive to the fact that participating in a group can be scary. Members wonder, "Will what I say be told to others?" "What will others think of my failures and struggles?" "Will they think less of me, or ridicule me?" A small group must be a secure place where participants trust each other and encourage each other. The no-slam rule (number 3) and ground rules like the following provide a good basis for this:

   a. Respect the privacy of each person. Do not repeat outside the group what anyone has said in the group.
   b. Do not try to "fix" others with the advice or suggestions you give. Instead, stick to your own experiences and insights, with great respect and an absence of criticism for the member who shares.
   c. Do not interrupt someone else as he/she shares.
   d. Talk about as much as you listen. Refuse to dominate or stay too quiet.

5. Use open-ended questions to encourage talking and thinking. An open-ended question requires more than a yes-or-no or pat answer. These open-ended questions work with almost every topic:
   • What do you think was the main message of this session?
   • What insights did you gain as you worked through this material before coming today?
   • What experiences did the author share that you can relate to?
   • What Bible passage relates to you most strongly right now? Why?
   • How will you live this passage?
   • How does this session bring you closer to living a life of integrity?
   • What issues surfaced as you studied that you know you need to address? How do you plan to address them?

6. Make it easy to share with strategies like everyone-around-the-circle-give-an-idea and speak-an-insight-in-alphabetical-order-of-first-name. When everyone shares in sequence, sharing becomes more comfortable and unanimous.

7. Lead the group in the "Encourage Your Group" activities as well as activities within the main text.

8. If your group gets sidetracked on issues other than that session's topic, jot these down and place them in the "Issue Bin," a box or paper bag you bring along. Then you can:

    a. Have an additional meeting just to discuss the issues listed.
    b. Meet a few minutes early the next week to tackle an issue placed in the box or bag.
    c. Suggest collegians talk these over after the study as schedules permit.

9. Close by prompting group members to complete the "Between You and God" section privately.

10. Close in prayer.

CrossSeekers Resources

To purchase CrossSeekers resources, please call 1-800-458-2772.
You may also obtain the resources by going to a LifeWay bookstore
or other Christian bookstore and using the ISBN number
provided with each resource.

Crossseekers Resources

CrossSeekers: Discipleship Covenant for a New Generation
by Henry Blackaby and Richard Blackaby

Discover the six CrossSeekers principles brought to life in a user-friendly, practical, story-telling format. This study sets the stage for an exploration of each CrossSeekers Covenant point. Biblical and contemporary examples of promises made, promises kept, and promises broken, along with consequences, bring the biblical truths home to today's college students.
• 9 sessions • Interactive in format • Leader's helps included • $8.95
• ISBN 0-7673-9084-9

Followology @ Collegiate Ministry: Following Jesus in the Real World
by Allen Jackson

How well do you follow as a Christian? *Followology* is designed for the college student or young adult who is serious about following Jesus. Through an informal, interactive study, collegians will learn to follow the One who knows the way, because He *is* the Way!
• 8 sessions • Interactive in format • Leader's helps included • $9.95
• ISBN 0-7673-9083-0

Transitions: Preparing for College
compiled by Art Herron

For high school juniors and seniors *and their parents*. Practical help for the transition from high school to college—the admissions process, financial aid, loans and scholarships, lifestyle changes, spiritual development, and more!
• 6 sessions • Leader's helps included • $7.95 • ISBN 0-7673-9082-2

CrossSeekers: Soul Food for Relationships, Developing Christlike Relationships
by J. Keith Miller

Our relationships with other people are key to happiness and success in life. Too often, though, these relationships become stressful and unhealthy. How can we keep them Christlike? J. Keith Miller examines the false personality we create that leaves us feeling lonely, fearful, doubtful. Confronting this constructed personality and dismantling the self-created aspects lead us to authentic living and Christlike relationships. This study supports the CrossSeekers Covenant point *Christlike relationships*.
• 6 sessions • Leader's guide included • $6.95 • ISBN 0-7673-9426-7

CrossSeekers: Spiritual Intimacy, Drawing Closer to God
by Glen Martin and Dian Ginter

Spiritual Intimacy will intensify the desire of your heart to know God more intimately, help you realize where you are in the process of drawing closer to God, and show you how to move ahead by knowing God on six successive levels. This study supports the CrossSeekers Covenant point *spiritual growth*.
• 6 sessions • Interactive in format • Leader's guide included • $6.95
• Available 4/99 • ISBN 0-7673-9427-5

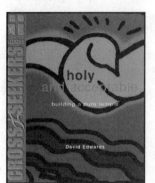

CrossSeekers: Holy and Acceptable, Building a Pure Temple
by Dave Edwards

First Corinthians 6 tells us that our bodies are temples of the Holy Spirit. But what does that mean, and why should we care? This study looks at what it means for us to be God's temple. Through Bible study and contemporary situations, the physical, mental, and spiritual aspects are explored, along with their interrelatedness, as well as what to do when you fail in your pursuit of purity. This study supports the CrossSeekers Covenant point *purity*.
• 6 sessions • Interactive in format • Leader's guide included • $6.95
• Available 4/99 • ISBN 0-7673-9428-3

CrossSeekers: Fearless, Sharing an Authentic Witness
by William Fay and Dean Finley

Fearless, Sharing an Authentic Witness will equip collegians for sharing their faith with others. Sessions address concepts such as our lives as a living witness (using the CrossSeekers Covenant points for discussion), how Jesus shared with persons He met, learning where God is at work in another person's life, a threat-free and effective method for presenting the gospel, and addressing difficult questions/situations. Based on *Share Jesus Without Fear,* this study supports the CrossSeekers Covenant point *witness*.
• 6 sessions • Interactive in format • Leader's guide included • $6.95
• Available 7/99 • ISBN 0-7673-9865-3

CrossSeekers: Gifted! Serving in Christ's Name
Gifted! Serving in Christ's Name examines spiritual gifts given by the Holy Spirit to each believer and leads collegians to discover their gifts and how to use them in service for Christ. A spiritual gifts inventory is included to enable collegians to determine their gifts. Collegians using their gifts in various service will be profiled, and opportunities for service will be highlighted. Collegians will be challenged to find a place of service utilizing their gifts. This study supports the CrossSeekers Covenant point *service*.
• 6 sessions • Interactive in format • Leader's guide included • $6.95
• Available 7/99 • ISBN 0-7673-9853-X

For more information, visit our Web site: **www.crossseekers.org.**